CHARRED RED FLOWERS

by
Palani Rajan

RAJAN»

First Indian Edition : August 2018
Copyrights © 2018 Palani Rajan
Price : Rupees 199/-

All rights reserved. This book may not be reproduced in whole or in part, in any form or by any means, electronic or mechanical, including photocopying, recording, or by any information storage and retrieval system now known or hereafter invented, without written permission from the publisher.

English Translation,
Cover Design,
Book Design
by

Rajkumar Palani B.E.

Printed and bound in India.

Rajan Publishers
18, Thatha Vathyar Street,
Kalaspalayam, Vellore,
Tamilnadu, India - 632 001
Mobile : +91-94432 27871

Dedication

To the loving memory of my dear wife
T.Hemalatha. B.Sc.,
(1952 - 2005)

Table of Contents

Review	3
PREFACE	4
Abundant Ambur	6
Assault on Police	10
Verdant Valleys	16
Communist Extremists	18
Hunt For Extremists	22
Who Is Seeralan?	27
Investigation	32
Government Enquiry	34
One Man Commission	36
Officials' Testimony	45
Constables Testimony	50
Officials' Nonchalance	53
Sessions Judgement	57
Creation Of Extremists	67
Assault On Koodapattu	77
Police Dragnet	82
Investigation	95
Wineyards	98
Practice Makes Perfect	101
Blood Lands	103
Peace Returns	105
Plight Of C.I.D.	106

-August 2018-

I am deeply indebted to all of my colleagues who provided valuable and timely information regarding the Jolarpet Naxalites.

Particularly - Late J.Bhaskaran D.S.P.(retd), Jolarpet Raju Constable(retd), Thirunaavukkarasu S.P.(retd), and now retired D.S.P.s Ramasamy, Henry Josef, Chinna Raj, Anna Durai, Sayed Imaam D.S.P.(Finger Prints), Late Selva Raj RSI(retd).

I would like to thank the Constables who helped investigate the Seeralan Murder - Head Constable Kaasi (2174), Constable Sivalingam (1902), Constable Rama Saamy (690).

In addition, my appreciations are extended to the Head Constable Subramani (who was assaulted by Naxalite Iruttu Pachchai) and TNJ-1111 Jeep driver Perumal. Hearty regards goes to Kodapattu, Kakkanaam palayam Govindasami Nayakkar and other general public who were hospitable to us.

Finally, I would like to salute our beloved Director General of Tamilnadu Police(retd) Mr.Davaram I.P.S., who evaluated this book and provided valuable feedback at this juncture.

R.Palani. B.A.,
Superintendent of Police(Retd),
Tamilnadu Police.

Review

W. I. Davaram I.P.S.
Director General of Police (Retd.)
President
Tamilnadu Athletic Association

Room No.81,
Jawaharlal Nehru Stadium,
Periamet, Chennai - 600 003.
Off : 2536 0203
Res : 2641 4194

My Dear Palani,

Received your letter dated 30th, may, only last week. Thanks a lot for providing such valuable data regarding the Naxalite movement in N.A. district before I was posted there in the year 1980.

The information will be very useful to me while writing about the Naxalite movement. If I need anymore particulars I will get in touch with you.

With best wishes to you and your family for a prosperous future.

Yours
Davaram

(22-6-2017)

PREFACE

Tenets of Chinese Communism:

1. Work according to your skills. Your family's needs will be fulfilled!

2. Except for the children in parents' lap, You can not claim rights over any property!

3. Oppressive and coercive regimes will slowly fade away.

These tenets faded away eventually even in China. With 53 out of the 270 super rich persons in the world, China stands first. These tenets are not being followed even in other former communist nations included Poland, Yugoslavia, Czechoslovakia, Romania, Bulgaria, Hungary, East Germany, Angola, Ethiopia, Somalia, Afghanistan, Cambodia, and South Yemen. Here in India, Communists are ready to whip themselves over their imaginary show of force, and trying to live their utopian dream.

Communism is against the principles of nature. The Communist revolution exploded in 1910 and spread all the way to China. But the revolutionary fervor eventually diminished. Positives and Negative forces balance out evenly in this world. Falsity is matched by truth, fearlessness is matched by cowardice, beauty is matched by ugly. Along the same axis falls the two qualities of wealth and poverty. Though they understand these universal principles sometimes men act like they don't understand this. Which is why he refutes the presence of infinite forces of Para-Brahma. Following communist principles is similar to the teenagers who commit suicide at the end of a "Blue Whale Challenge" online game.

Till the judgment day comes, the reality of leading an oppressive life is the reality we all face and die. At the same time, people will lead a secret shady life and will be punished for that offense. Do we need this sort of a life? Russia relaxed its communist ideology and started following Socialism. But China - did not heed the clarion call of nature and its people - is steamrolling Chinese citizens freedom with its oppressive policies.

The seeds of this poisonous ideology were brought to India and sown here by the Bengali Manibendranath Roy. He traveled to Russia, after the 1917 Russian revolution and spread it in India. This ideology sprouted fast in Andhra. When F.V. Arul Inspector General of Police was serving in South Andhra, a gang of Communists, after firing shots looted a Jewelry shop.

The names have been changed to protect the involved persons in this true story.

~ 1 ~
Abundant Ambur

During the Sangam period, Tamilians known as 'Aravar' by Telugu people, lived in the proximity of the town 'Aamoor'. 'Aam' stands for clear spring water in ancient Tamil. This ancient name Aamoor in the course of time changed in to Ambur.

From 1976 to 1982, the tranquil Yelagiri Hills situated next to Jolarpet in the vicinity of Ambur, became a raging revolutionary volcano and erupted with bloody consequences. The concomitant incidents obvisouly affected the life of the general public, challenged the wit and intelligence of Tamil Nadu Police Force in ways unknown before, and Yelagiri Hills-folk was caught in the midst of a bloody revolution. The blood spilt caused crimson flowers bloom in those serene hilly climes. The facts and true incidents behind how those crimson blossoms came about, wildly multiplied and eventually wilted are captured and compiled in this slim volume.

Yelagiri Hills is situated nearby the town of Jolarpet. Standing tall at 4,350 ft. it hosts of clutch of 12 quaint villages. The village folks are unassuming and modest people. In contrast to them, the people who lived at the foot of the mountain are known for their shrewdness and worldly wise ways.

Ambur was a small town by any standards in the year 1976. Ever crowded and packed with streaming automobile traffic is the Chennai - Calicut highway, passes through Ambur. From ambur one can drive to the towns of Krishnagiri, Hosur and to the city of Bangalore. The town limits begin from Veera Koyil that lies east of the Ambur and stretches all the way to 'Minnoor' and 'Maaraa Pattu'.

Hemming the two sides of the road are evergreen trees of Tamarind, Palm, Punnai, Pungan and Marutham. Bountiful Mother Nature, omnipresent in the form of large coconut groves were keeping the town breezy and pleasant. Overlooking the town are the hovels of Hindus, Muslims and Christians, lined the road behind the O.A.R. movie theater. These hundreds of hovels impart a shanty town look to the whole area. Whilst crossing over 'B-kaspa', mixed fragrance from the flowers - Jasmine, Iruvaatchi, Mullai, Thaazhampoo, Thavanam and Samanthi - gently caresses our nostrils. All the above flower varieties are extensively cultivated in this area by small farmers.

Going further, are the Nallathambi Dispensary, Muslim High School, Taluk Police Station, a few mechanical workshops, and a Petrol Bunk. Situated next is the Salaam Hotel which brings aromas in the air, pierces one's nostrils and evoking the memories of Muslim Biryani cooked over hardwood fire. Patrons of Salaam hotel, will park their cars and lorries along both sides of the main road and will be dining on the plentiful and delicious biryani. Customers will exit the salaam hotel, only after packing their biryani parcels to take home with them.

People will hurry to take their vehicles after braving the upset constables berating and their whistle blast.

Opposite to the salaam hotel is the Modern cafe run by a Tamil Brahmin. Next is the M.A.R. Lodge, Vellore based A.S.A. Bakery's Ambur Branch, and Sri Talkies. Opposite to the bakery, are seven to eight small shops with thatched roofs. Shops include Police Informer Muhammed Ali's bicycle repair shop and sundry small shops actively engaged in their businesses. Whatever happens in Ambur town, that information will reach the sharp ears of Muhammed Ali. Shortly he will pass on that intelligence to the Town Police and Taluk Police and facilitate in their law and order activities. Located to the North is the Police station road. Going up the Police station road there is Government Medical Hospital, Police Station, Magistrate Court, Municipal Market, tenements of Ambur towns folk in the form of buildings and tiled houses.

To the south of the main road lies the Railway station road, seems always bustling with traffic. Inside the Railway station premises is the Travelers' Bungalow, that lonely stands among the tall green teak trees. Huts of Muslims are also present near the Travelers' Bungalow. Saandror Kuppam, Somalaa Puram, Aalang Kuppam and Periyan Kuppam are nearby villages of Ambur. At Aalang Kuppam main road, near Nehru statue a tea shop is run by Thangavel Mudaliar in his hut. Opposite to the tea shop, there are two Jameen palatial houses and Jameen agricultural lands.

South Indian Tannery and the T.A.Abdul Vaaheedh Tannery are located at Peryaan Kuppam main road - these two leather tanneries manufacture colorful leather products. Ladies handbags, shoes, sandals, leather jackets and pants, gloves are manufactured and exported to the developed countries like Russia, Japan, Germany etc.,. There is no dearth of daily wage jobs in this area.

Tanneries, Beedi factories, Coconut mandis, Rope mandis and Jaggery mandis make sure their workers are content and lead their peaceful life. Minnoor has a Tannery run by the Tamilnadu Government. From the hind quarters of minoor village, Aalang Kuppam, Soloor, Saandror Kuppam by the mud roads one can reach the arable lands of Ambur. There amidst the Sugar cane fields, lies Ambur Police circle office.

~ 2 ~
Assault on Police

Ambur police circle office area wore a deserted look for a greater part of the day. This mud road traverses for 30KM till Palli Konda. There is a Circle Inspector, a writer, and a constable for office help in this Circle Office. Office help leaves for lunch daily at 1 P.M. sharp.

On the day of 30 September 1976, at 2 P.M. as usual, Circle Inspector Venketachalam pushed his scooter to go for lunch. Writer Desingu, scurried towards the scooter and snapped to attention and saluted. Desingu watched the Circle Inspector leave the office.

Writer Desingu was the only person present in the Office. After Inspector left, he washed his face and hands and prepared to have his lunch. Desingu could see that in the distance there were two persons coming towards the circle office in a bicycle. The cycle was pedaled by a fair, skinny person and a short stout person was riding in the pillion. At that time it was an offence to travel in doubles using bicycles. Writer Desingu Rajan intercepted them by waving them down.

"Hey you both there, Stop the Bicycle!! What a Nerve to ride in doubles in front of the Circle Office?" Twice Desingu slapped them both in their back.

Bicycle came to a Halt. The Pillion rider muttered "Please Forgive us, Sir!" and proceeded to stuff a Five Rupee note in the hands of writer Desingu. In the Magistrate Court for Doubles offence the standard fine is merely three rupees per head. Since they offered him five rupees Desingu got suspicious. He rolled the bicycle in to the Circle office premises and parked it there. The black guy stuffed another five rupee note in Desingu's hand. By now Desingu was just about sure that something is not right about these two fellows.

Desingu after punching them in their back once, ordered them to empty those two bags hung in the cycle and show the contents of the bags. Since they did not heed to this order, Desingu attempted to examine the bags by himself.

Immediately the fair skinned person from his pant pocket whipped out a "Pitchuva" stabbing knife and stabbed forcefully above Desingu's hip. Stabbed constable Desingu groaned loudly and fell down. Both the cyclists ran in to the sugarcane fields and then ran towards Devalapuram and disappeared. Wounded Desingu yelled "Aiyo, They stabbed me!! They stabbed me!! Catch them!!!".

Hearing these loud cries, around 5 farmers rushed from the nearby Sugarcane fields to Desingu's help. They bandaged Desingu's wound with a piece of cloth. Desingu was bleeding badly. Desingu rang up the
Ambur Town station and called police men for his aid.

A head constable and a few constables present in the Ambur Town Police station came to circle office along with a cycle rickshaw. They carried Desingu to Ambur Government Hospital located near by the Ambur town station and admitted him in the hospital for treatment. Ambur Town Police Inspector hearing the news came back to his office. The two bags left by the cyclists were lying in the floor in his office. He examined both the bags. One bag contained a shirt, a lungi, and a Communist book titled "Gangaiyil irunthu Olga varai" (From Gangega). In the other bag was a shirt , a lungi and two country made bombs wrapped in thick twine and a few Gelatine sticks.

Inspector Venkatchalam ordered his men to register a F.I.R. (Ref: Ambur Town P.S. Cr.No: 1236/76 U/S 307 I.P.C. r/w 286 I.P.C.). in the Ambur Town Station. He also made sure the two country bombs were placed in two separate water buckets safely. Then Inspector Venketachalam messaged the District Superintendent of Police, and Superintendent of Police(Q-Branch CID)

Circle Inspector Venkatachalam directed all the constables to search nearby villages for the escaped assaulters. General public started assembling in front of the Government hospital shouting that "Police has been stabbed!!, Police has been stabbed!!". The police asked the crowd to disperse but was in vain. Three-Star Lorry owner Ismail, cycle shop Muhamad Ali, Modern Cafe Iyer, Ex-M.L.A.s Sambangi, Panner selvam visited Desingu in the hospital and consoled him. For further treatment Desingu was sent to Government Pentland Hospital in Vellore.

Q-Branch Deputy Superintendent of Police from Madras, Inspector Henry Joseph, Sub-Inspector R.Palani visited and enquired the stabbed Desingu in the Government Hospital on that very day.

Since Desingu Rajan was transferred recently from Vellore Armed Reserve to Local Police, He was not that familiar with the Police processes and procedures. He said that the Fair skinned lean person stabbed him. He further said that before asking their names and their addresses the cyclists stabbed him. The identity of the assaulters was not known. For the next six months Police searched for the assaulters in many places. Could the police catch the extremists easily?

Q-Branch Sub-Inspector R.Palani tried to find out how extremists came in to the possession of country bombs. He investigated whether anyone from the retired Madras Engineering Group men in the district of Vellore taught the extremists about bomb making. He found that the M.E.G. was started during Queen Victoria's reign. At that time only three retired officers of M.E.G. were alive and even they were very old.

It was later found that country bombs were manufactured by Naxal extremists themselves and they distributed the bombs among themselves as per their needs. While manufacturing these Country bombs, two extremists - Tamilarasan, Amballi Muniraasu- were apprehended in the town of Jeyankondam. country bombs were made out of Gun Powder, Sulphur, Charcoal powder mixture.

Bicycle wheel bearing balls are embedded inside bombs with a wick attached. The wick is sandwiched between two match box strips along with a match stick. A thread is tied to the match stick. When the thread is pulled, the match stick burns, lighting the fuse and the bomb explodes.

Q-Branch Sub Inspector R.Palani also wanted to find out how the extremists came in possession of gelatine sticks. He along with the Head constable R.Selavaraj checked around 200 Explosives material dealers(Gun Powder K-License Holders and gelatine sticks and Detonators L-Form License Holders) present in North Arcot District. Besides this, He visited Perambattu a nondescript town located in the border of Dharmapuri - and checked the records of Explosives dealers in their godowns.

Dealers of explosive materials get their licenses from Vellore Collector office. When a farmer intends to dig a well in his land they need gelatine sticks to break up the rocks. So they approach the officials in Vellore Collector office and get permission to purchase up to 25 gelatine sticks. With the permission in hand they buy the sticks from the L-Form godown owners. This process is valid only once for a farmer.

In the Collector office they maintain a ledger listing out which farmers from which taluk got gelatine sticks permission. L-form owners visit the Collector office and get that list under the table. Then they illegally sell the gelatine sticks to whomever pays the highest price.

If you analyse their daily transactions book they would have sold to the same five persons repeatedly for more than 100 times. If you find and enquire the concerned person about this malpractice he will say that he bought gelatine sticks only once for digging a well. And that too, he will clarify that he bought gelatine sticks but from another dealer altogether.

In Chetti Kuppam of Gudiyattham, two brothers - ChakraBani and SarangaBani indulged in such license abuse for many thousands of times. They amassed wealth and agricultural lands and built and lived in palatial houses and enjoyed an extravagant life. Q-Branch Sub-Inspector detected this fraud while investigating about the explosives Supply Chain of extremists. He immediately alerted the Vellore Collector Office and requested the cancellation of their licenses. This clandestine supply chain was used by the extremists for their violent purposes came to light and all dealers were reined in.

3
Verdant Valleys

To the North West of Pachur village in Nattram Palli area and near the outer most of Southern Andhra, located are the Kuppam Hills. Palar originates as a small stream and joins the overflowing waters of Lake Petha Managalam in Karnataka. It then merges with the springs of Madha Kadappa at Vaniyam Badi, Malattaru, Mitta Palli, Mathina Palli and Sarangal rivers of Umarabad, Pernampat. It then intermingles with Gudiyaththam Moredhana River and takes shape as the Great Palar. At that time, Palar floods atleast once a year, touching both the banks when it reaches Vellore.

The parallel hill ranges of Jamuna Maraththur and Yelagiri starts from Aalangayam and touches the villages of Koodapattu, Poongulam, Mittoor, Irunaapattu, Perumapattu, Kurisilaapattu, and ends at Thirupathoor. The valleys between the two ranges and the towns located on the other side of Yelagiri near Vaniyambadi, Jolarpet were very fertile. Clouds often gather on top of these two hill ranges and caresses each another and it rains often due to convection. The region is packed with fertile lands that grow banana, coconut, sugarcane, paddy and harvesting happens here thrice a year.

Just like Ambur, jaggery mundi workers, beedi mundi workers and leather shop workers were in great numbers in Nattrampalli, Jolarpet. The towns also had its share of rich and wealthy among its populace. Vaniyambadi had many rich Muslim merchants, Jolarpet had Sun beedi, Rajan beedi factory owners, Thiriyalam mittatharars, and a few wealthy reddiyaars. Alangayam had AVK Bus owners, Bakthavachalam Reddiyaar of Mittoor, and Srinivasa Reddiyar were very wealthy landlords at that time.

In the dense forests of Jamuna Marathur, trees of Teak, Ahil, Sandal, Jackfruit, Kadambai, Rosewood, Vengai and Redwood were in spades. Gangs roamed these forests to chop down these valuable trees and smuggle them to other states. They were an audacious lot and will stop at nothing. Many of them were convicts released or escaped from jail sentences. If extremists hide themselves in these forests or in the hundreds of acres of coconut and mango tree groves, no one can locate the extremists for years.

Mullai Vadivelu and Mullai Sakthi were brothers and they were very rich. Besides they nurtured the political party - DMK - in this district. Their Mango groves were famous back in the 1950's even. DMK chieftain Anna Durai, and other political leaders lodged in the farm house of their groves. Their daily needs and sundry were supplied by the Mullai brothers' household. There were hundreds of such mango groves in the twin districts of Vellore and Dharmapuri.

4

Communist Extremists

In 1967 CPI party broke in to two with CPI(ML) as one faction. Chaaru Majumdhar, Kanu sanyal, Jangal Santhal were leading the break away faction. From CPI(M), an extremist faction calling themselves as "Marxist and Leninist" broke away. On 18-May-1967, Communist extremist leader Chaaru Majumdhar along with his armed supporters launched an assault on a village called "Naxalbari" in the state of West Bengal. There he murdered many landlords and rich farmers besides killing BSF police. Then the state of West Bengal was under the Government led by Communist leader Jyothi Basu. So the West Bengal police were averse to the idea of arresting Charu Majumdhar. Charu Majumdhar was travelling everywhere in broad day light without any imminent arrest fears. The same Charu Majumdhar later died in Alipur Jail on 28 July 1972.

In the year of 1975, India was under the iron grips of Indira Gandhi's emergency. To escape from the fury of the emergency the Communist extremist of West Bengal sought refuge in the southern most peaceful state of Tamil Nadu. The Communist sympathizers of Dharmapuri rolled out the welcome wagon and embraced them. Then the State of Tamil Nadu was under the freewheeling regime of D.M.K. In a similar manner the North Indian Communist leader George Fernandes was also shielded from emergency in Tamil Nadu.

Charu Majumdhar Naxalites secretly camped in the districts of Dharmapuri and Vellore and brainwashed poor farmers with their Communist propaganda. Jolarpet's many beedi factory workers were also susceptible to this malevolent propaganda. In the town of Thirupathoor, Advocate Bakthavachalam MA.BL. was nurturing the nascent Communist party. Killing rich landlords and eliminating their families were all in a day's work for Communist extremists. Their goal was Armed Revolutions brought to bear in the districts of Dharmapuri, North Arcot and South Arcot. To that end, Communist extremists gathered their local leaders in the forests of Jamuna Marathur, Ponneri of Jolarpet and conducted classes on how to successfully execute Armed Revolutions (Do away with). These classes were scheduled under the cover of darkness in the middle of the night in these forests and desolate groves without the knowledge of general public.

Charu Majumdhar faction tutored and created local Communist extremists like Dharmapuri Nayakan Kottai Tamilvaanan, Ko.Gopal.MA., Marameri Kannamani, Dharmapuri Balan, Arasampattu Karnal, South Arcot Tamilarasan B.Sc., Jolarpet Sivalingam, Saminathan, Seeralan, Nedun chezhiyan, Kanagaraj, Gunalan, Ammaiyappan, Varadhan, Elumalai, etc.,. They later set to work in Jolarpet circle with the intention of murdering big farmers who pay unfair wages, loan sharks, and mitta-miraasus. They were determined to eliminate whoever comes as an obstacle to their deadly goal.

Communist extremists groups were mostly comprised of persons who are unsatisfied in their life. People who are dirt poor, those who resent their caste they were born in, lumber jacks, beedi workers, those who strayed from family life, practicing lawyers, educated rogues were the majority.

A.M.Kothandaraman M.A.B.L. (aka AMK) of Anaimallur in North Arcot district, was leading the Communist extremists of Tamil Nadu. He was already in hiding. In the district of South Arcot, a Communist extremist gang made up of Vathiyar Kaliya perumal, Arumugam, Thimmakaali, AnanthaNayaki, Ko.Gopal set out to murder a rich landlord. They sent one of them to work in the landlord's farmhouse so that he can subdue the guarding dogs. They entered in to the farm house in the midnight and murdered the landlord. When the public went after them they lit and threw firecrackers to distract and dissuade the pursuants and escaped.

Five of them, later caught by the Tamil Nadu Police, after conviction with life sentences, were jailed in the Vellore Central Prison. Post 1976, some Communist extremists were smuggling grenades that were made in China and were supplying them to the Communist extremists of Tamil Nadu. The very same Communists were funding the activities of Communist extremists of Tamil Nadu. It was believed counterfeit Indian currencies were being supplied from China for their extremist activities and even their legal expenses were borne by the Chinese Communists.

Communist extremists started carrying a grenade for attacking and self defense purposes. Till that time - in the district of Dharmapuri - such crimes were not registered as extremist cases and considered as activities of regular Communists. In Dharmapuri, vibrant youngsters like Tamilvanan, Sidhdhananthan, Munirasu, Balan, Kannamani, Panneer selvam, Karnal, Ko.Gopal were attracted by the Communist ideologies and joined the Communist extremists party. On 8 February 1973 they murdered Dharmalinga chettiyar in Paroor. In a similar manner in 1976 they murdered Appasami chettiyaar in Nagarasampatti, Mathoor. They lit and threw fire crackers to intimidate pursuants and managed to escape unscathed.

Tamil Nadu's capital city of Madras were also affected by these extremists and Police were actively looking for Communist extremists for setting metro buses on fire, attacking the All India Radio station, etc.,. Naxalites were also searching for their comrade L.Appu accusing the state Police as the cause of his disappearance. They might be searching for him even now for all we know.

5

Hunt For Extremists

The year was 1976. Q-Branch was working non-stop in search of Communist extremists in the northern Tamil Nadu region. In North Arcot district's capital Vellore, Q-Branch office was manned by Inspector Henri Joseph, Sub Inspector R.Palani, Head constable R.Selvaraj, constable Gopal. They were investigating the case of deadly assault on Ambur constable Desingu and were on the lookout for the Communist extremists involved.

Once Q-Branch Sub Inspector R.Palani went to an informal meeting with the Jolarpet Sub Inspector J.Bhaskaran to discuss the latest criminal developments in the Jolarpet area. Bhaskaran shared with R.Palani an important information about some strident youngsters in Ponneri, Yelagiri foothills of Jolarpet. These youngsters had formed themselves in to a group and were menacing the farmers in that area to pay higher wages for agricultural workers. Around 10 farmers refused to heed to their threats. As an act of retribution, these youngsters invaded the lands of these 10 farmers in the night time, chopped down and damaged all the banana trees. (Ref: Jolarpet P.S. Cr No.1062/76, 1096/76, 1097/76, 1144/76 U/S 147, 148, 341, 448, 427 I.P.C etc Cases)

Even though this looked like a simple case of labor dispute, Bhaskaran was convinced that these were none other than Communist extremists. Bhaskaran also informed R.Palani that one Sivalingam - an absconding criminal - was the one who is instigating these youngsters.

Q-Branch Sub Inspector R.Palani recognizing this significant tip-off from J.Bhaskaran and immediately passed on this information to his higher-ups namely - Inspector Henry Joseph and Deputy Superintendent of Police Ramasamy. Then they also intimated the office of Q-Branch Superintendent(Madras) to take this matter further. A team was formed to enquire about the whereabouts of the absconding criminal Sivalingam. After many days of enquiry the team came to know that Sivalingam was in-fact an employee of Indian Railways as a rail engine driver and that he belonged to the Vakkanam patti area in the Jolarpet main road.

The team was able to find that in 1973 there was a clash between the two neighbouring villages of Vakkanampatti and Kodiyoor. Sivalingam along with all the involved men in the above clash were brought to the Police station for enquiry. Deputy Superintendent Dharmaraj came to Jolarpet police station for enquiring the clash. During enquiry Sivalingam stabbed a person suddenly while all of them were watching. The team also found that Sivalingam was subsequently charged with attempted murder (Jolarpet P.S Cr No 37/73 U/S 147, 148, 151, 152, 332, 426, 427, 448, 224 I.P.C.) and was convicted with one year imprisonment. Sessions Court reduced the sentence to six months. Sivalingam was an active member of the political party - DMK. Sivalingam appealed in High court but one year imprisonment sentence was re-instated by the High Court. Sivalingam moved Supreme Court but the one year sentence was confirmed there. As a consequence of this crime and resultant conviction, Sivalingam lost his rail engine driver job. There after Sivalingam jumped bail and went underground.

Even though such sporadic incidents were occurring in the North Arcot district, armed uprisings were unheard of till 1976. According to the political theory of Marxism–Leninism, the "Kulaks" (tightfist-ed affluent peasants) were class enemies of the poorer peasants. Vladimir Lenin described them as "bloodsuckers, vampires, plunderers of the people and profiteers, who fatten on famine". Russian Government officials violently seized kulak farms and killed resisting farmers while others were deported to labor camps. Fueled by this Communist Propaganda, rich farmers who refused to pay higher wages as demanded became a natural target for these armed revolutionary gangs. These gangs started meeting in the foot hills of Ponneri and drew up an action roster. The roster consisted of selected persons like Sivalingam, Saminathan, Kathirvel, Shanmugam, Senkodi, Kanagaraj, Seeralan, Ammaiyappan and Nedunchezhiyan.

The villages and hamlets in the foothills of Yelagiri were really fertile. Due to abundant rain fall, bumper harvests were the norm in those villages. The clan of Reddiyaars were very prosperous and were mainly agricultural land owners with forty to fifty acres of fertile lands. Impelled by these Communist precedents the armed revolutionaries shortlisted top ten affluent farmers in that area for attacks. Days later they put their plan in to action and destroyed all the banana trees in those ten banana groves.

Jolarpet Police were unable to corner this revolutionary gang. Even though the gang members roamed in plain sight in front of Jolarpet police no one stepped forward to identify them. Reason was all the people in Jolarpet and surrounding villages are mostly Vanniya Gounders. They were also related to each other and were cousins and nephews of the gang members.

Constable Appu - a native of Jolarpet - was with the Q-Branch then for Special duty. The extremists who came to know about this, one night approached the two milking cows tied in front his house and poisoned them. Because Appu was also not a Vanniya Gounder but belonged to Otta chettiyar caste.

Another constable with the Q-Branch was Raju. He belonged to Vanniya Gounder caste of Jolarpet. Raju knew almost all of the extremists by way of family relations. In the beginning even Raju was tending to his Q-Branch Police duties with disinterest. But when Deputy Superintendent of Police Ramasami promised a job in the Police force for Raju's son, Raju began to sing. He pointed out one extremist after another in Jolarpet area with out hesitation.

To solve the banana groves destruction cases, and apprehend the extremists, hundreds of Police men formed in to many teams and conducted raids in all the surrounding villages under the name of "Storming Operations". All the Communist extremists who were involved in the banana groves destruction to threaten landowners skipped the town of Jolarpet and went in to hiding.

The Communist extremists traveled to many towns by bicycles in pairs to villages populated with beedi workers, match factory workers, and Communists. These towns and villages included Gudiyaththam, Chetti Kuppam, Pachur, Kurisilaapattu, Nattrampalli, Thirupathoor, Koodapattu, Mathoor, Kadhili, Sundarampalli, Vengalaapalli. Many Communists in these towns and villages patronized these wanted extremists and helped them in many ways.

6
Who Is Seeralan?

The Q-Branch Police suspected that one of these roving Communist extremist pairs must have stabbed the Ambur constable Desingu. Q-Branch is a branch in Tamil Nadu Police specially tasked with monitoring extremists. Normally a Q-Branch team will visit two villages daily by bus to reconnoiter and gather latest developments about these extremists. They are empowered to enter suspect villages in the mid nights using lorries and conducted house searches often.

Thirupathoor advocate Bakthavachalam M.A.B.L. was attracted by the Communist Ideology while he was in college and joined the Communist party. He incited the general public to file cases against the Police department by cooking up charges and projected himself as a leading advocate. He blew up Seeralan incident and organised public meetings with local Communist leaders, M.L.A.s like Umanath and his wife Pappa umanath, Journalist Maithily Sivaraman as speakers. They launched a vilifying campaign against the Police.

"Police men are scavengers of dead meat, hunting dogs!!!"

"Police are stooges of the Ruling class!!!"

"Police men work 24 hours a day. So enter their houses in the middle of the night. Sleep with their wives!!!"

Above is a sampler of their vituperative verbal attacks against Police in these meetings. Bakthavachalam had a brother by the name of Ramanujan who was also a popular Communist in Thirupathoor town. He owned a big chicken farming business in Asiriyar Nagar in the outskirts of Thirupathoor.

In search of these extremists around 150 Armed Reserve Police, Q-Branch officers and local Police formed many teams and combed the forests and groves in this region.

extremists encampments like Gandhi gramam, Ponneri, Mandalavadi, Kaveripattu, Vettapattu, Arasampattu, Sundarampalli, Veerapalli, Vakkanampatti Kodiyoor, Kudiyanakuppam, Ramanur, Chinna Kammiyampattu, Chandrapallam, Kethandapatti were raided by the Police teams once a week. In response Communist extremists started to shift their meeting spots often to escape the Police dragnet. extremists identified new places as their encampments and recruited new members to their cause. The new recruits were taught to eliminate rich farmers, kill loan sharks, terminate whoever stands in their way, destroy farmers who pay unfair wages, attack higher officials of the Government.

Athipallam of Puthupet in Nattrampalli range, is the native of Velu, a farmer. He built a hut in his agricultural land. He lived in that hut and also minded the farming. He was literate and a Communist sympathizer too. He taught himself siddha medicine by reading books and was offering first aid and treatment of wounds for

Communist extremists. The extremists of Jolarpet met him often and brainwashed him with Communist ideologies. This information came to the ears of the villagers and they informed the Q-Branch office about this as well. To collect more information about the persons who are meeting Velu often, Q-Branch office deputed three constables namely 1. Head constable Kaasi (2174), 2. constable Sivalingam (1902) and 3. constable Ramasami (670).

The three plain clothed constables kept watch for two days and they were uneventful. On the third day 22 Apr 1978 at 12 Noon, Velu after finishing all his farming chores left his house. A short while after, the constables saw two persons enter Velu's house. The constables approached Velu's wife Jeya and enquired about the visitors. Jeya replied in the negative. The plain cloths men asked her about the two pairs of sandals that were near the entrance of the house. Jeya became evasive and the constables like a shot, barged in to the hut.

The two suspects inside the house were startled by this entry and pushed the constables aside and took to their feet. Constables gave them a chase and rounded them up. One suspect hurled a country bomb on the constables and it hit the wall of Velu's house and exploded with a loud bang!! Shrapnel flew everywhere!!

The wall developed cracks and constable Sivalingam was hurt in face from the flying shrapnel. The shaken and hurt constables recovered their composure and tried to subdue the two accused. Two constables got one accused down and tied his hands behind his back with a rope.

The other accused was vehemently pushing the hurt constable Sivalingam in to a big well without parapet wall. Hurt from the explosion, constable Sivalingam yelled out for help. The other two constables rushed to the spot and beat the attacking accused and saved constable Sivalingam. Injured from the beatings the accused collapsed down. Using this commotion the other accused whose hands were tied started running and disappeared beyond the hills.

Upon hearing this scuffle and yelling around fifty villagers had assembled near the spot. One of the villagers phoned the Nattrampalli Police station and informed about this scuffle. The three constables picked up the collapsed accused and hog-tied him to a yoke and brought him to the main road. Then they lowered the yoke and placed the accused on the road.

Q-Branch officers were the first to arrive at the scene and they examined the accused. The Officers found the accused to be dead. Then they informed the three constables that it was not proper procedure to move the dead body from the spot and advised the constables to restore the dead body to the spot. The dead body was taken back to the spot and placed near the well.

The identity of the dead accused was not known to anyone. In the Natrampalli Police station this incident was recorded as suspicious death (Ref: 25/77 U/S 286, 302, 307 IPC) and registered two First Information Reports (F.I.R.s) (26/77 U/S 286, 307 IPC). A copy of this F.I.R.s were dispatched to then Thirupathoor Sub-Collector Ramu I.A.S.

7
Investigation

Hundreds of townsmen who came to know of this untoward incident has gathered in to a crowd. Darkness in its sinister form began to cover everything. All the activities of the villagers came to a stand still and the whole village froze. Plain cloths men and uniformed Police men poured in to the village in Police vehicles. At sharp 6.30 PM, Thirupaththoor Sub Collector, Vaniyambadi Tahsildhar, Thirupaththoor Tahsildhar, along with their assistants arrived. Q-Branch men were busy working out the identity of the dead man from the acquired body marks of the corpse and they thought it could be one Seeralan. So they have already sent two constables to Ponneri fetch Seeralan's father from his native village of Gandhi gramam.

By then it was too dark to see and two petromax lanterns were brought over. From the nearby house electricity was drawn and two bulbs were installed to adequately light up the scene.

Vaniyambadi Tahsildhar collected the witnesses and Panchayathars and produced before Sub-Collector Ramu. Seeralan's father after examining the face and body of the corpse asserted to the Sub-Collector - "This is not my baby!!". Some more men were brought over to identify the corpse but may be due to the swollen and blood stained face no one was able to positively conclude its identity.

Sub-Collector in front of the witnesses and Panchayathars completed his inquiry and ordered the body be sent to the Thirpathoor Government Hospital for autopsy.

The very night Sub-Collector returned to Thirupathoor. Next day morning, Q-Branch Sub Inspector R.Palani, collected finger prints from the body in Hospital mortuary using the appropriate official forms and arranged them to be sent to Magistrate Court. He also requested the magistrate finger prints be forwarded to Finger Print division for further analysis and sent a copy to Sub-Collector. Magistrate ordered the finger print division to analyse them and submit their findings to the court.

8

Government Enquiry

Thirupathoor Sub-Collector ordered next day to announce this news by using tom-toms throughout his range and request information from the public regarding this incident. A week later around 50 persons came and offered their testimony. Butcher Saththaar Khan, Communist lawyer and People Rights Party leader Bakthavachchalam, his brother Ramanujam, and some more witnesses from the near by villages were produced by Communists.

A week later Sub-Collector inquired them all and recorded their testimonies. Velu, Jeya, Durai samy, Nedunchezhiyan were considered as prime witnesses. Police side produced witnesses were - involved constables Kaasi, Ramasami, Sivalingam, Q-Branch Inspector Henry Joseph, Thirupathoor town Inspector Kannan, Vanyambadi Inspector Janardhanan, Thirupathoor D.S.P. Veera Pandiyan also tendered their testimonies. Finger prints expert D.S.P. Sayed Imam was also enquired.

Sub Collector Ramu I.A.S. sent the results of his enquiry to the Government as a report. Based on the report Tamil Nadu Government issued orders to suspend constables Kaasi, Ramasamy, Sivalingam, Inspectors Henry Joseph, Kannan, Janardhanan, and D.S.P. Veera Pandiyan.

After two months the Government ordered to investigate this case in a proper manner and instituted a one man commission headed by Srinvasan I.A.S. (Revenue Board Member No.I). Srinivasan was not new to this area as he already worked as a District Collector in Vellore district in 1962.

⚖ 9 ⚖
One Man Commission

Next month Srinivasan I.A.S. arrived in the town of Thirupathoor. The Enquiry was conducted in the premises of Thirupathoor Sub Collector office. Communist lawyer Bakthavachchalam appeared in the Seeralan's side and retired assistant public prosecutor No I Tiger Varadhaachaari represented the Police side. We can't help but mention the resourcefulness of retired assistant public prosecutor here. The following is a true incident that unfolded before the author's eyes while the court is in session.

Before the year of 1971 illicitly distilling arrack was a criminal offence and Tamil Nadu Police were arresting the illicit arrack distillers and sellers. In one such illicit distilling case, the retired assistant public prosecutor was questioning witnesses in front of the court. The distilling mud pots and pipes seized were introduced as exhibits in the proceedings.

This distilling apparatus structure consisted of 3 mud pots placed one above the other. The bottom pot is where the fermented wash will be heated. The middle pot has a hole in the bottom to let the vapors in and collects the condensed vapors. The top pot contains cool water that has to be changed often to maintain the proper cooling temperature. The mud jar that was on display for taking out the warm water from the top pot was too big to enter in to the top pot. In the middle of questioning the witnesses the retired public prosecutor noticed that the mud jar was too big to enter the top pot and immediately deduced the opposition lawyer will argue that distilling couldn't have happened with these pots.

In a flash of a moment, asking "Is this the Jar?" he took an about turn towards the witness and while turning he crashed the mud jar against the witness stand. The jar shattered in to dozens of pieces and he managed to secure the face of the prosecution side that day. Thus, he was a master in out-maneuvering the opposition and winning his cases in one way or another.

Now for the benefit of the lay reader we would like to explain about evidences, witnesses and Indian laws governing them in a few short paragraphs.

Evidence is that testimony or material that proves, or tends to prove, a specific fact. The first action of an incident or occurrence begins the generation of various forms of evidence, depending on the incident or occurrence. The key to proving the elements of a cause of action is obtaining and preserving key evidentiary objects and artifacts. Evidence generates suspicion, key facts, and proves or disproves the elements of a case.

It begs the questions of what the evidence is telling the investigator, that is, how does it speak to the investigator, and what story is the evidence telling the investigator about the incident or occurrence.

Three kinds of evidences were laid down in ancient Hindu texts like Vasishtha Dharmasutra.

"Likhitam Sakshino Bukhti Parmanam Trividham Smritham"
1. Lekhya (Document), 2. Sakshi (Witnesses), 3. Bukhthi (Possession).

A witness, has been a key player in the pursuit of justice delivery. The fundamentals of justice necessitates that the truth and impartiality must be quintessence of justice. This brings the role of an onlooker as witness to confirm or report to criminal justice agencies the ingredients of the incident.

Regular witnesses testify according to the five senses: what they saw, heard, touched, tasted, or smelled. They are normally not considered as an expert witness, and their testimony is most often limited to factual matters surrounding a case.

Chapter IX titled "OF WITNESSES" of the Indian Evidence Act, 1872 consists of seventeen Sections spreading from Sections 118 to 134 deals with
1. Competency;
2. Compellability;
3. Privileges; and
4. Quantity of Witnesses required for judicial decisions

Sections 118 to 121 and Section 133 of this Act provide for competency of witnesses whereas Section 121 (Judges and Magistrates) and Section 132 (Witness not excused from answering on the ground that answer will criminate) refers to the compellability of the witnesses.

Armed with the above knowledge, we invite the reader to join us in the upcoming legal argumentations.

So the big day came finally like a rushing train. Q-Branch Sub Inspector R.Palani woke up early, got ready and reached the Sub Collector's office, well before the proceedings began. The early morning air was damp and chilly. As the hours went by all the lawyers, witness, officials began to arrive one by one. Shortly there after thousands of inquisitive general public started to gather in front of the Thirupathoor Sub Collector office. Hundreds of uniformed police men and plain-cloths men encamped in a fire station in front of the Sub Collector office.

Q-Branch Sub Inspector R.Palani was seated inside the enquiry hall and was taking notes from the testimonies of the witnesses. Periodically he was sending his notes and information to Q-Branch - Madras head office with the help of a V.H.F. wireless set.

Board member only allowed assistant public prosecutor and the communist lawyer to sit in the audience and watch the proceedings. Reason was Communist lawyer was asking leading questions and assistant public prosecutor was interjecting those leading questions. Communist lawyer Bakthavachalam and his assistant, lawyer Chandran were parading as heroes in front of the one man commission while the police side was manifestly preoccupied and wringing their hands.

Once a week Tiger Varathaachchaari came from Vellore and participated in Srinivasan Commission. Special branch Sub-Inspector Perumal, finger print expert Sayed Imam and 15 other constables came from Vellore in a Police Van to motivate the police side for seven continuous weeks. Food and miscellaneous expenses for them and 50 more police men were sponsored by the Nattrampalli Head constable Kaali.

"ATHTHIPALLAM VELU!!!,
ATHTHIPALLAM VELU!!!,
ATHTHIPALLAM VELU!!!"

called out the Sub Collector Caller for three times. Velu appeared before the Board member and said "I swear to tell the truth, the whole truth, and nothing but the truth".

Lady typist of the Sub Collector typed the notes as Velu started deposing.

"I am a Communist Sympathizer. Me, my wife and my kids are living in a hut built on our own land. I can speak and write Tamil. I have interests in Sidha medicine and Communist Ideologies. On the day of the incident, at 11 AM I drew water from the Kavalaibari well and watered my paddy crops. Then I left for Nattrampalli to buy goat meat. I purchased goat meat and vegetables in

Natrampalli market and returned to my hut at 1 PM. There three men were hog-tying a dead man to a yoke."

"My neighbors informed me the three men were police constables. Around 50 villagers had gathered in the spot by then. The whole village was silent and came to a stand still. The three constables carried the dead man towards the main road. At 3 PM the same three constables returned the body back to the spot near the well. At 4 PM, lots of police men arrived wearing khaki shorts, in uniform and in mufti. Thirupathoor Sub Collector and his assistants arrived at the scene at evening 6.30 PM."

"Since it was dark by then, they drew electricity from my hut and hung light bulbs. Even then there was no adequate light at the scene and so they brought two petromax lanterns. All the witnesses were called in front of the Sub collector and Tahsildhar and they enquired all the witnesses. Police brought a couple of witnesses to the spot and asked to identify the dead man. But no one was able to identify the body positively. Sub Collector sent the dead body to Thirupathoor Government hospital for autopsy. Sub Collector enquired me regarding this matter."

"One day when I was passing by the Thirupaththoor Court, I was called in to the Thirupaththoor town police station. Inside the police station were present four officers with Vellore Q-Branch Inspector Henry Joseph. Taking turns they attacked me with their bare hands. Henry Jospeh tortured me by pricking all over my body with an office pin. He lit a cigarette and burned me with that in many places. He tied me to a tree and let big ants all over my body to bite. They beat me asking on the day of the incident who are all the men that came to my house. Then they took me by a Jeep and confined me for twenty days. I could not recognize the place where I was kept. They fed me for twenty days and beat me daily asking questions. I marked the wall of the lockup cell with a stick - twenty lines for twenty days."

Communist lawyer Bakthavachchalam was making hand gestures to Velu while he was deposing. The assistant public prosecutor noticed this non-verbal communication between the two and opposed these actions strongly.

"VELU'S WIFE JEYA !!!,
VELU'S WIFE JEYA !!!,
VELU'S WIFE JEYA !!!"
called out the Davali.

Jeya took the witness stand and offered her testimony as follows:

"On the day of the incident, my husband worked the fields and watered the paddy crops and rested in our hut for sometime. After 11 PM he left to town for purchasing goat meat and vegetables. I was the only one in the hut. After a short while, I heard loud noises and I peeked outside. Three men were fighting with one man."

"I was told that the three men were police constables. Three constables thrashed the other man and he fainted. His face was completely bloody. They pressed a yoke on his neck. By then my husband returned back from town."

"It looked like the fainted man was already dead. Two constables hogtied the body and carried it off. Then they returned the body to the spot next to our well. At 4 PM, the same day lots of uniformed and plain clothed police men arrived at the spot. After it turned dark, Collector came and enquired me and my husband. Then they took the body to Thirupaththoor hospital. Then one day when I my husband was in Tirupaththoor, police took him in to the station and tortured him by pricking with pin, burning with cigarettes and biting ants. They locked him up for twenty days and then they released him. I gave my statement to the Sub Collector."

After Jeya's deposition, Ponneri Duraisamy - father of the dead man Seeralan - was called to tender his testimony.

"I live in a Yelagiri foothills village Gandhi gramam. I work as a line inspector in Tamilnadu Electicity Board. I was issue less for ten years after my marriage. Seeralan was born after that. Even though he was a mischievous kid, he did not have any bad habits while growing up. He was a good man. He had lots of friends in the village of Ponneri."

"On the day of the incident, a few constables came to my house in the evening. They informed me that a person was dead in Aththipallam village near Velu's house. They asked me to come to the spot and identify the body. I grew nervous and went to Aththipallam with them. When I arrived it was dark and there laid a corpse near a well."

"They pointed the corpse to me and asked to identify if that was my son - Seeraalan. Sub Collector, Tahsildhar and many police men were present on the spot. I was completely baffled by the situation. The face of the dead body was drenched in blood and was swollen. So I told the police that - THIS IS NOT MY BABY. I came to know later that it was indeed my son. Police accused my son wrongly and they killed him unjustly."

All the testimonies scheduled for that day were over.

Next week Nedun chezhiyan - Seeralan's father's brother and a Communist extremist, a few females and many others deposed. They were produced before the one man commission by lawyer Bakthavachchalam and his brother Ramanujam. The week after that some expert witnesses and finger prints expert Sayed Imam were called for deposing.

Sayed Imam produced records about two prior convictions of Seeraalan and that he was convicted for stealing Indian Railways properties. He also established and produced documentary evidences regarding Railway Protection Force's criminal history sheets for Seeraalan.

✒ 10 ✍

Officials' Testimony

Next week the one man commission called for Q-Branch Inspector Henry Joseph, Police Inspectors Janaardhanan, Kannan, constables Ramasami and Sivalingam.

Inspector Henry Joseph deposed in English while others deposed in Tamil.

"I have been working in the Q-Branch from the year 1975. Then there were no Communist Extremism cases registered in North Arcot district. By the fag end of the year 1976, Ambur circle writer was stabbed by two extremists and escaped, leaving behind two bags with two country bombs, gelatine sticks and communist literature on a bicycle."

"From that incident only we came to know of large Communist extremists presence in the Jolarpet area. They were present in many parts of Jolarpet and Dharmapuri. Their influence were felt in Kolar Gold Fields, Andhra kuppam, Pachur, Kandhili, Sundrampalli, Saamalpatti, Arasampatti, Maththoor, Nayakkan Kottai, Ottapatti, till Gudiyaththam - and even pervaded the hills, forests and groves."

"In the last quarter of 1976 we were accounting for extremists' actions in the district of North Arcot. In 1975 - at Sundarampalli - a Nayinaar was marked as a loan shark by a group and a murder attempt was made on him using dangerous weapons like scythes and sickles. In that incident Jeeva, Manali and a few colony youngsters entered the village limits and hid in darkness and enacted their deadly act."

"The criminals involved in that above incident are still absconding. Near Thiruvannamalai, on the Villupuram border in the village Avoor they murdered a wealthy landlord by sending one among them as a servant in the landlords' house and so that he can subdue the guard dogs and let the murder gang in to the house. Involved criminals like Nondi Shanmugam and Koththagutta selvam are still in hiding."

"In Jolarpet, Sivalingam, Seeraalan, Saminathan, Natarasan, Nedunchezhiyan, Ammaiyappan and 10 others got together and destroyed thousands of Banana trees in the lands of Bakthavachchala Reddiyaar and 10 other big landowners."

"Even though the accused were said to be absconding in the Police records they were freely going about their life without any arrest fears. Reason was no one came forward to identify the criminals. Besides they traveled by deserted footpaths near railway lines to many villages and spread Mao-Tse-Tung's principles among the villagers. Their ultimate aim was to create extremists in these villages and make them join their armed struggle. We came to the conclusion that one of these pairs stabbed Ambur writer Desingu. Many villages in the ranges of Jolarpet, Natrampalli, Kandhili, and many villages in

Dharmapuri like Paroor, Arasampatti, Ottapatti, Maththoor were searched by conducting sudden raids in early morning hours and day times."

"These searches yielded many clues to the police and one important information we came about was about Velu of Aththipallam, Puthupet of Nattrampalli range. Velu was entertaining suspicious visitors and we wanted to know details about those visitors. So for the task, we picked three special duty constables - physically well built Ramasami, courageous Sivalingam, and Head constable Kaasi. We ordered the trio to keep watch on Velu's hut and if they come across any suspicious visitors they were to apprehend them and bring back to us."

"On the third day of their watch, while capturing two persons the three constables were attacked with country bombs. One fellow escaped while tying them down. Another accused attacked constable Sivalingam and the other two constables went for his aid. A struggle ensued between them and Sivalingam lost one of his teeth. The captured accused was tied to a yoke and brought to the main road."

"While I was in Thirupaththoor town station I heard the news in V.H.F. wireless set. Immediately while going by Puthupet main road, I saw the three constables and the injured accused. While I examined the fainted accused I found out that he was already dead. I informed the three constables about this death and advised them to restore the body to the spot. Then I left."

"Afterwards it occurred to me that the dead man's features looked similar to that of one Seeraalan in the records. So I quickly dispatched some constables to Ponneri to bring Seeralan's father to identify the body. Since the spot was dark by then, I asked the Natrampalli Sub Inspector to arrange for electric lights and petromax lanterns. When these arrangements were complete Thirupaththoor Sub Collector along with Tahsildhars arrived and took stock of the situation. He gathered the witnesses and panchayathaars and conducted the inquest."

"Duraisami brought over from Ponneri also inspected the body and its face. But he stated that 'This is not my baby!' in English. The corpse was sent to Thirupaththoor Government hospital for autopsy. There the finger prints from the body were collected and submitted to the Sub Collector. They were routed by the court to the finger prints division for further analysis."

"Later I sent a report to Q-Branch Police Superintendent Chandra Mowleeswaran stating that - Seeralan was Ponneri Duraisami's son. Seeraalan has a criminal history sheet in the Jolarpet Railway Protection Force Police station. Seeralan was an old criminal under the watch of police department."

Thus Inspector Henry Joseph completed his long winded but interesting testimony.

Then the Davali called out thrice.

"VANIYAMBADI INSPECTOR JANARDHANAN !!, VANIYAMBADI INSPECTOR JANARDHANAN !!, VANIYAMBADI INSPECTOR JANARDHANAN !!"

Janardhanan appeared before the commission and stated,

"I heard this news in V.H.F wireless set while I was attending another matter in Vaniyambadi. Then I collected my constables and reached the village of Aththipallam at 3.30PM. I advised the Sub Inspectors and constables regarding this incident. Then I made arrangements for the enquiry to be conducted by Sub collector. I was temporarily suspended from the police duty. Other than this I do not know anything about the Seeraalan's incident."

Next was the testimony of Thirupaththoor town Inspector Kannan.

"I am working as Thirupaththoor town Inspector. I came to know about Seeralan's death from the V.H.F. wireless transmission. Inspector Henry Joseph was with me when I heard this news. Me and Henry Joseph visited the spot seperately. I dont know anything more about this incident."

ॐ 11 ॐ

Constables Testimony

"CONSTABLE SIVALINGAM!!,
CONSTABLE SIVALINGAM!!,
CONSTABLE SIVALINGAM!!"

Davali called out thrice.

Sivalingam took the witness stand and stated as follows

"I served as a Special duty constable in the Q-Branch. One day Q-Branch Inspector called me, Ramasami and Kaasi for capturing two suspicious men visiting Aththipallam Velu's hut. The three of us kept surveillance for two days non-stop. On the third day around mid noon we saw two suspicious men enter Velu's hut. We went near Velu's hut and asked Velu's wife Jeya about Velu. She said that Velu has gone to Puthupet. So I asked her to whom the two pairs of sandals lying outside the hut belonged to. Since we didn't get a satisfactory reply from her the three of us entered her hut."

"Two men pushed us aside and ran outside the hut. When we tried to capture them, one of them assaulted us with a Country bomb. In the bomb explosion the wall cracked and I was hurt in the face. We three caught hold of one accused and we rolled on the floor trying to subdue them. Head constable Kaasi and constable Ramasami got together and tied the hands of the dark looking accused.

The other accused was trying to kill me by pushing in to the kavalabaari well."

"In one of the punches I received from the accused one of my front teeth broke and went missing. I yelled to ramasami for help. He along with the Head constable rushed to my aid and saved me from the attacking accused. We three hogtied the captured accused to a yoke and carried him to the main road. Villagers gathered and helped us. I asked one of the villagers to ask the Natrampalli Police to inform Q-Branch Inspector via V.H.F. wireless set. Around 2.30 PM Q-Branch Inspector reached us and after examining the accused he advised that he is dead already. So he advised us further to restore the dead body to the spot near the well. Then he left."

"Then restored the body the scene and waited for the police. In a short while, Vaniyambadi Inspector, Natrampalli Sub Inspector, Thirpaththoor Inspector, Thirupaththoor Deputy Superintendent of Police and many constables reached the spot. While it was about to become dark, Thirpaththoor Sub Collector, Thasildhaars arrived at the spot. Then they conducted inquest and sent the body to Thirpaththoor Government Hospital."

"Tamilnadu Government has suspended me regarding this incident."

Thus Sivalingam finished his testimony.

Head constable Kaasi and constable Ramasami gave their testimonies and they closely resembled the testimony of constable Sivalingam.

≫ 12 ≪
Officials' Nonchalance

Next week, the Doctor who conducted autopsy on Seeralan's body appeared to depose. He explained the identification marks on the body, the nature of the wounds sustained by Seeralan before his death. His deposition was over. The week after Board member came to Thirupaththoor and conducted an enquiry.

The first to depose was BalaKrishnan, the Superintendent of Police of North Arcot district. In his deposition he mentioned that Vaniyambadi Inspector Janardhanan sent a report about the dead person in the above incident. He said that he forwarded that to C.I.D. office and to the Inspector General of Tamil Nadu. The board member clarified his doubts by asking couple of questions to BalaKrishnan. BalaKrishnan replied as follows:

Board Member: "What did you mention as the dead person's name in the report you sent to the Government?"

S.P. BalaKrishnan: "I mentioned it as Srinivasan."

Board Member : "What was the name of the dead person mentioned by Inspector Janardhanan in his report?"

S.P. BalaKrishnan: "He mentioned it as Seeralan s/o Duraisami."

Board Member : "Then how did you mention the name as Srinivasan instead of Seeralan?"

S.P. BalaKrishnan: "I dictated the names to my camp clerk. He typed it incorrectly as Srinivasan instead of Seeralan."

Board Member : "Are you the one who signed the report incorrectly typed by camp clerk?"

S.P. BalaKrishnan: "Yes!"

Board Member : "Did you read the report before signing it?"

S.P. BalaKrishnan: "Yes!!"

Board Member : "Then why didn't you point out the mistakes and ask to correct it?"

S.P. BalaKrishnan: "It was my mistake!! Please don't record it!"

Board member did not reply to BalaKrishnan but noted down all the replies of BalaKrishnan including that it was his mistake. Then he asked BalaKrishnan to sign that document.

Superintendent of Police BalaKrishnan became anxious and started to sweat profusely.

Then Q-Branch Superintendent Chandra Mowli took the witness stand and started deposing. In his deposition he stated that he composed a report about the incident based on a report sent to him by Q-Branch Inspector Henry Joseph. Then he said that he forwarded his report to Inspector General of Police and Government of Tamilnadu.

The following were the questions put forth by the Board member:

Board Member : "By what names did you mention the dead person and his father?"

S.P.Chandra Mowli : "I mentioned them as Seeralan s/o DuraiVelu"

Board Member : "What were names mentioned by Q-Branch Inspector in his report to you?"

S.P.Chandra Mowli : "He mentioned them as Seeralan s/o Duraisami"

Board Member : "Then how did mentioned it incorrectly in your report?"

S.P.Chandra Mowli : "I dictated to my camp clerk correctly but he typed it wrong."

Board Member : "Did you read that incorrect report before signing it?"

S.P.Chandra Mowli : "Yes."

Board Member : "Then why didn't you point out the mistake and get it corrected?"

S.P.Chandra Mowli : "Yes. It was my mistake. Please don't record it!!!" He pleaded the Board member.

Board member did not utter a word but recorded all his replies and got the statement signed by Chandra mowli.

Chandra Mowli stepped out of the witness stand and said "My stomach is upset!!!" and rushed to the Traveler's Bungalow. Board Member completed his enquiry and traveled back to Madras.

13

Sessions Judgement

With the next two months, Tamil Nadu Government on the basis of Board member enquiry filed a case in the lower court. Assistant public prosecutor (I) of North Arcot - Krishnaiyyar - registered a prima facie case without cross examining witnesses in Thirupaththoor S.M.Court where the Magistrate allotted PRC (Preliminary Register Case) number. In this case the District Collector was marked as the complainant.

Krishnaiyyar mentioned the reasonable grounds, found in the witnesses' depositions for accusing three police officials, and three constables, for collusion in the killing, screening the evidence and wrongful confinement. He filed the charge sheet in the Vellore Sessions court in sections 302 IPC 201, IPC 344, and 120(B) IPC r/w 109 IPC through the Sub Magistrate.

Sessions judge Pakkiri Shankar, allotted SC(Sessions Case) number and then took the case for hearing. Witnesses were served with summons and produced before the court. The police officers and men now stood as accused.

On the first day of the case, lawyer Bakthavachchalam appeared on behalf of murdered Seeraalan and explained that he belonged to an armed revolutionary force. The lawyer demanded in a threatening tone that this case ought to be conducted keeping in mind that Seeralan fought and gave up his life for this country (Martyr) and that he was unjustly murdered by the police. He further eulogized Seeralan as a Brave man and an action hero. The Government lawyer on whose shoulders rested the responsibility of conducting this case remained silent.

The police accused's side was represented by Vellore's experienced and leading crminal lawyer V.Varadharajan, Tiger Varadhachchaari and Salem's leading criminal lawyer Meenakshi Sundaram. D.S.P.Veera Pandiyan was represented by a leading criminal lawyer from Madras.

To help the Government lawyer, renowned criminal lawyer of Vellore A.K.Thandapani and Thirupaththoor Bakthavachchalam filed a Vakkaalath (Power of attorney given to a Lawyer for conducting a case). But Justice Pakkirishankar ordered the duo can help the Government lawyer within legal bounds but should not interfere in the proceedings.

All the lawyers were unanimously of the opinion that the very talented V.Varadharajan should be the one to conduct the case.

Varadarajan stood in front of the bar and explained that Seeralan was not a Martyr but a thief. He was involved in many theft cases. To praise Seeralan is an act trying to mask the fact that he is a thief. Lawyer Bakthavachchalam is playing scare tactics by trying to frighten this court. But the court will rise above such petty tactics and establish the truth. All the lawyers present inside the sessions court clapped their hands loudly and welcomed this argument.

Since the murder of Seeralan was a case that rocked the nation, most of the leading lawyers practicing law in Vellore were present inside the court. They were watching the proceedings of the case very attentively.

Q-Branch Sub Inspector R.Palani, was seated next to the lawyers representing the police accused. He was clarifying their doubts, as and when they raised them, about the places, names and order of the events. R.Palani was also passing notes and hints with the help of paper slips to the lawyer Varadarajan, who stood arguing in front of the judge. Varadajan intelligently incorporated those hints passed to him, in his arguments and in cross examining the witnesses.

Witnesses started their depositions while sessions judge's typist Desigachchaari started typing rapidly.

One after another the witnesses deposed just like they testified in the one man commission. Varadarajan cross examined all the witnesses and overwhelmed them with his cross questioning. At last, it was D.S.P.(finger print) Sayed Imam produced documentary evidence regarding the fact that Seeralan was a convict in two prior cases and stated that Seeralan's criminal records are actively maintained by the Railway Protection Force. Then came the medical officer who conducted autopsy on Seeralan's body and gave his testimony. Vardarajan let him walk freely without any questions.

Sub collector Ramu I.A.S. came to depose next and in his deposition he explained all the details about the enquiries he conducted regarding this case. Varadarajan rose to cross examine the Sub Collector Ramu. He approached the Collector and gently asked him

"What is your name?"

Sub collector replied hurriedly "I have already explained all the details about me to the court!!" and refusing to answer the above question.

Varadajan shot back loudly

"I AM HERE TO ASK YOU ONE THOUSAND AND ONE QUESTIONS. YOU MUST ANSWER THEM!!!".

The assembled lawyers in the court clapped their hands loudly and welcomed Varadarajan. This made the Sub Collector loose his composure and his face grew ruddy. He wiped the sweat on his forehead and started replying indiscriminately.

Varadarajan : "Who is Seeralan?"

Sub collector : "Seeralan is a Communist."

Varadarajan : "Seeralan is a thief. He stole properties of Indian railways and was punished twice. Did you come to know about this fact?"

Sub collector : "Yes."

Varadarajan : "Then why didn't you describe Seeralan as a criminal in your first deposition?"

Sub collector : "Because I thought it was not necessary."

Varadarajan : "It was said that the witness Velu was wrongfully confined for 20 days? He also mentioned about the 20 markings he left on his cell. Did you visit the police stations to check for those markings?"

Sub collector : "Velu's relative filed a 100 Cr.P.C petition and checkup were conducted in all the cells. But we came to know all the cells were only recently whitewashed for inspection."

Varadajan completed cross examining all the witnesses.

In his argument Varadarajan explained to the court that Seeralan attacked constable Sivalingam with so much force that Sivalingam lost one his teeth in his attack. Varadarajan added that more over he pushed Sivalingam in a well with the intention of killing Sivalingam. Varadarajan cited many judgments to stress that in Section 100 IPC - which says it is not a crime to defend oneself from an attacker with murderous intentions. It further goes to say that killing such an attacker is legal as well.

Also he said that accused are incriminated with destroying evidences under 201 I.P.C. He said that this is factually wrong. The accused thought that Seeralan was alive and carried him off to the main road. Then only they came to know that he was dead and restored the body to the spot. He argued that how can this act be considered as destroying evidences? He pointed out the folly in their accusation.

D.S.P. Veerapandiyan's Madras lawyer conducted his arguments to the extent that the D.S.P. should be acquitted. Varadarajan argued for all the accused. Varadarajan placed an important notion in front of the court. That is he acted as an exponent in explaining the nuances of 100 I.P.C.

In - Jaidev Vs State Of Punjab - the Supreme Court has observed as follows:

"There can be no doubt in judging the conduct of a person who proves that he had a RIGHT OF PRIVATE DEFFENCE, allowance must necessarily be made for his feelings at the relevant time. He is faced with an assault which causes a reasonable apprehension of death of grievous hurt and that inevitability created in his mind some excitement and confusion. At such moments the upper most feeling in his mind would be to ward off the danger and to save himself and his property and so he would naturally be anxious to strike a decisive blow in exercising of his right."

Again he insisted the same 100 I.P.C. in different manner in different angle. In case of Gurlingappa Sidramappa the Bombay High court has delivered the judgment as follows:

And in the judgment (Bombay Law Review 817 (22) Cr L.J. 618 (1921) A.I.R B 335 (B) and in the case of Siddappa (1952) Hyderabad 52, (1953) Cr L.J 1141)

"Whether the apprehension was reasonable or not is a question of fact. The weapon used, the manner of using it, the nature of assault and other surround circumstances will be taken into account"

Thus the Supreme court and the High courts state:

"It is not illegal to kill a person who is attacking with intention to kill. Further it says it must be examined that which weapon was used in the attempt to kill and which method was used to kill. In the Seeralan case, Seeraalan and his comrade attacked the police men with a dangerous bomb. The walls are damaged in that attack. Explosives expert from Madras examined the crime scene and has certified that the explosives were used in that attack on the police. The accused were struggling to escape from the bomb attacks by Seeralan. They were struggling under the situation that already a bomb has gone off injuring one of the accused. The honorable judges should take these facts in to account. "

Further the accused were said to have wrongfully confined the witness Velu. To establish this the prosecution failed to provide any evidences and supporting witnesses in front of the court.

Section: 100 Cr.P.C. describes:

"Whenever any place is liable to search of inspection under this chapter, is closed, any person is residing in or being in charge of such place shall on demand of the officer or other person, executing the warrant and so production of warrant allow him free ingress there to and offer all reasonable facilities for a search there to"

Varadajan added further that Velu's side has filed a petition under 100 Cr.P.C. and many prison cells in the police stations were examined for those markings. But no evidence was found to prove Velu's accusations. In this situation the question of Wrongful confinement doesn't even arise.

Velu accuses that he was attacked by four to five officers in Thirupaththoor town police station, Henry Joseph burned him with a cigarette, pricked all over his body with pins, let ants to bite. Who are all those four to five officers? why they were not produced in front of this court? He failed to mention which of them hit Velu in which part of his body. But accusing blindly is like fixing the blame on wrong persons.

Prosecution did not even lift a finger in the direction of identifying the other 4 officers. Velu accuses he was confined for twenty days. Which town or village was it? Which police men took him there? How did he go to that place of confinement? By bus? or by Jeep? What is the number of that vehicle used for transporting Velu to his place of confinement? Who are the men who gave him food for those twenty days? Why all these men were not identified by conducting identification parades?

Why the Sub Collector who conducted the enquiry didn't exhaust efforts to identify these men? Why witness Velu haven't identified or point out any constable or officer till the end?

Vardarajan rattled off the above questions and more non stop. The prosecution lawyer Mogambari was unable to reply to these questions asked by Varadarajan. Mogambari laconically replied that the evidences furnished already should be sufficient. The Court was adjourned for judgment.

On the judgment day, Judge Pakkiri shankar read out his judgment. He said that after hearing the arguments of the both the Government and Accused sides, he offered the benefit of doubt to the accused and released all the accused.

Lawyer Bakthavachchalam appealed the case in Madras high court. The case was dismissed. Bakthavachchalam went to Supreme Court and even to Central Human Rights Commission.

14
Creation Of Extremists

Communist Motto:

1. No Hero Worship

2. Don't trust in bragging paper tigers.

3. Do away with the hurdles to Communism.

4. Take the people's problems and struggle for them.

5. Join other parties and stress the Communist principles.

6. Join other parties and trouble them.

Who ever supports the above Communist mottos are the true blue Communists.

The wealthy swindling the poor workers, loan sharks charging exorbitant interests, distress due to slander about their tainted character, insufficient income, occupational slump, disgrace due to familial quarrel are some of the causes that make people to lean towards Communism.

Back then these frustrated lot cannot become members immediatley in the Communist party. First they will be taken in as Communist Sympathizers. These sympathizers will undertake the ground work for conducting public meetings. Then printing wallpapers, pasting them on the walls of the town, going street by street and collecting funds for the meeting expenses were the nature of low level jobs they must undertake and perform them satisfactorily to the leaders.

Then they will be elevated to the next level. They will be appointed as information couriers while sharing secrets and messages between the party's underground leaders. Then they are expected to cultivate their courage in challenging the defaulters in street brawls etc.. Then they put to practice these skills in the villages they live and their places of work. These are the nascent Communists.

Now the Communist extremists will assign small criminal actions for them to successfully execute. Then they will involve them in big crimes like murder and extortion, driving them in to underground finally. Thus they will be isolated from the general society and will turn in to full time extremists.

But in the present days, they turn in to full fledged extremists from day one.

In Ambur Police circle Inspector office two accused came by bicycle and stabbed the writer Desingu and escaped. They left behind their bicycle, two bags containing country bombs, gelatine sticks, and Communist literature. Local police and Q-Branch were unable to solve this stabbing case and the case was pending investigation. The police were faltering in handling the case of killing a dangerous Communist called Seeraalan. After that case came to a conclusion, the police turned their vigil towards the Communist extremist pairs roving village after village in lone bicycles.

After managing Seeralan's case, Balakrishnan - Superintendent of Police, Vellore - offered a Jeep to the hither to traveling by bus or hiking Thirupaththoor Q-Branch officials. The Jeep driver's father-in-law lived in the third house to that of extremist Sivalingam. So the Police Jeep was able to keep watch on Sivalingam's house under the guise of visiting Jeep driver's father-in-law's house. The fact that extremists Natarasan and Saminathan's houses were also located next to that house worked out in the Police favor to keep watch on them.

In Kodiyoor of Jolarpet, extremist Gunalan who was a relative of Pinang house. He was passing by the lands next to his house on 12 Oct 76 at 5 PM. A Bomb he was carrying was accidentally triggered off and exploded while he was holding it. In the explosion his right forearm got severed and was blown off. Hearing this news, Jolarpet Sub Inspector Bhaskaran, Thirupaththoor town Sub Inspector Thirunaavukarasu, and Q-Branch Sub Inspector R.Palani formed a team with some Police men. They surrounded his house at gun point and searched for clues and evidence. But the search failed to turn up anything useful to the police.(Jolarpet P.S. Cr No 1217/76 286 I.P.C. R/W 338 I.P.C)

Jolarpet police took the injured Gunalan to the Vellore Government pentland hospital for treating injuries of explosion. The Q-branch men enquired him later for hours who were all involved in the Ambur stabbing case. But Gunalan stubbornly refused to reveal the details about the stabbing.

In 1977 Pachur of Natrampalli, there was one Sadik Basha, considered to be in touch with the Communist extremists. Q-Branch Inspector Henry Joseph arrested him and lodged him as a detenu under the N.S.A. for a year. In that same prison the extremist convicts of South Arcot Pennadam case - 1. Vathiyar Kaliya Perumal, 2. Thimmakkaali, 3. Arumugam, 4. Anantha Nayaki were also lodged. Along with them was the Communist extremist Ko.Gopal M.A., convicted in the Dharmapuri case.

The Q-Branch was tasked with censoring the correspondence of these Communist extremists with the outside world. Once while censoring Ko.Gopal's letters they came across the following lines.

Gopal writes to his Mother:

"I am imprisoned behind the jail bars. Here it is drizzling and looks like it will soon begin to rain heavily. The rain drops are piercing the red earth like just released arrows. This falling rain and the soil intermingles and produces an earthy aroma. This gives me boundless happiness and reminds me of the days I spent in our house in our village."

It is normal for the reader to think of extremists' nature as cruel and vicious. But their other side is very soft and they even feel and enjoy the wonderful nature. It pleasantly surprised the Q-Branch men tasked with censoring.

In the district of Trichy, there was a village called as AyuthaKalam. There Communist extremists like Tamilrasan, Amballi Muniraj, etc were secretly making country bombs in their house. The local police were tipped off about this illegal bomb manufacture and stormed the spot and arrested them. The Q-Branch Police men belonging to all the districts participated in enquiring them. One of the extremists named Muniraasu started brainwashing a Head constable. "You have left your home and roaming the country side just like us to catch extremists. What did you achieve so far? Join our side, we will pay you double the amount you receive now as salary.!!!"

But Munirasu during enquiry he refused to part details about his movements. Tamilarasan and Munirasu were lodged in the Trichy Central Prison. The height of the prison compound wall was 11 feet. Both these extremists manage to scale this tall compound wall and escaped from the prison. Police found out they were missing and searched entire Trichy town on the same night.

In the early morning hours the escapees were caught by the general public. Tamilarasan was seriously wounded. They were immediately transferred to the Vellore Central Jail. One day the Inspector General of Tamil Nadu E.L.Stracy was visiting the Vellore Central Jail and saw the injured Tamilrasan. Stracy enquired him about his injuries. Tamilrasan rudely replied "This is the work of your men only. Mind your business and get lost!!!" Stracy was embarrassed to take the conversation further. Stracy realized that the saying "Hurt snakes should be left alone" is very true.

To trace out Communist extremist's activities and locations many informers who pass information to police regarding illegal acts must be appointed in every town and village. Only intelligent Inspectors and Sub Inspectors are capable of identifying potential informers and can appoint them. Government allocates funds for informers in every financial year. It even earmarks funds for appointing informers who monitor Communist extremists. But those funds never reach beyond the Gandhi statue in Madras Marina Beach. Officers will phone the sub ordinate officers daily and enquire the day to day progress. How can they show growth and progress? First, quality informers should be identified and appointed. Then they must be met with often and harvest crucial information. In such meetings it is advisable to part with cash amounting to at least Rs.50 (a decent amount in the late 1970s).

Because of the failure to appoint informers the Police department was unable to bring the Communist extremists under control in the late 70s. The department should have let a constable to appoint at least 10 informers with the funding of Rs.50 per informer. If there is a financial crunch in funding then the criminal informers should be promised, reduction of their sentences or remove criminal offenses in their names.

The higher officials should enquire their sub-ordinates once a month about the appointment of their informers, location and their tasks they have undertaken. Looks like the Britishers took all these police tactics with them while they left this country for good. Because of the dearth of informers, balance of power looks tilted in favor of the criminals and extremists from Kashmir to Kanniyakumari.

North Arcot Q-Branch Inspector Henry Joseph was transferred from his position and a rank promoted Inspector Krishnasami took the reins of Q-Branch in North Arcot.

Q-Branch Sub Inspector R.Palani was determined to show progress in the Ambur writer stabbing case. He took with him Head constable Selvaraj and searched for bicycle shops in villages like Kandhili, Thirpaththoor, Jolarpet, Vaniyambadi, Ambur, Gudiyaththam, Sundrampalli, Madavaalam, Perampattu, Vishamangalam and many other villages. He met with more than 100s of Bicycle repair shop owners and enquired them for clues in the above case.

He also brought them over to the Ambur Court and showed them the bicycle left behind by the extremists who stabbed the Ambur constable. He enquired in particular whether they have repaired that bicycle or a bicycle like that one. But many bicycle repairmen replied in the negative.

Sub Inspector R.Palani and Selvaraj put in many months of work in enquiring bicycle repairmen in all the neighboring locations. One day constable Raju informed Sub Inspector R.Palani, there was an electrician in a Church located in the road from Jolarpet to Kaveripet and that he also repairs bicycles. R.Palani and Selvaraj visited the church and sought for the Church electrician. They found the electrician the next day and immediately they took him to the Ambur court to identify the extremist's bicycle.

Sub Inspector R.Palani showed Stephen the bicycle that was under remand and enquired him whether he knew the owner of the bicycle. Stephen without hesitation replied "This bicycle belongs to Vakkanampatti Sivalingam!!". Stephen further added that he had repaired the same bicycle many times. They collectively heaved a sigh of relief and took Stephen back to Jolarpet and dropped him at his house.

Ambur local police were handling the investigation of Ambur writer Desingu's stabbing case. Therefore the Sub Inspector R.Palani informed Ambur local police that Desingu was stabbed by the duo - Vakkanampatti Sivalingam and Seeralan. He further asked Ambur local police to conduct an Identification Parade to confirm that it was Sivalingam who was involved in the stabbing.

When Desingu was asked to identify Seeralan's body, Desingu could not identify the body or the face because the face was badly swollen and bloody. So the Sub Inspector R.Palani composed a report to higher officials that it was indeed Sivalingam and Seeralan were the ones who stabbed Desingu and confirmed that fact.

After Seeralan murder case, people were found to be in a state of high arousal in villages like Ponneri and Mandalavadi. Reason was lawyer Bakthavachchalam and his brother Ramanujam were instigating the people to publicly oppose the Police force. Bakthavachchalam was a Communist lawyer, only in name because he milked money even from the Communists - big sums in the name of legal fees. He was charging the Communists more than what other lawyers would, when it comes to Communism related cases.

Thirupaththoor Communists, lawyer Bakthavachchalam, Communist snitch Sathar Khan, and many others organized meetings, processions in places like Santhaimedu of Thirupaththoor, Jolarpet, Ponneri. The processions were in daytime and the meetings were conducted in the night times by the Communists. Leftist Indian express reporter Maithili Sivaraman, sitting M.L.A. Pappa Umanath participated as special speakers for the second time.

As usual they attacked the Police force as "Rabid Hounds, Wolves, Carcass feeding Vultures!!!" to their heart's content. Many communists spoke at length about the ruling class and their atrocities. Bakthavachchalam appeared in the stage intermittently and acted as a comic relief by roasting the police force. For example he ridiculed constables that they mark in their notebooks as they worked for 24 hours a day for the sake of travel allowance. The gathered mass clapped their hands and had a good laugh.

Madras Q-Branch Inspector Ramasami was promoted as a Deputy Superintendent of Police. He was appointed for the post of Q-Branch Deputy Superintendent for the Vellore range. After he took charge the Q-Branch men showed more passion in their work and produced some good results.

15
Assault On Koodapattu

Ponneri was a Communist extremist camp. Vaniyambadi to Thiruppathoor main road has got a parallel mud road goes along the foot hills of Yelagiri. Using this mud road one can reach many villages like BalnangKuppam, Thamal Eri Muththoor, Pakkiri Tharkka, Venagayapalli, Gowthampettai, Madavalam, Jalagam parai and the Jalagam Parai water falls. If you cross all these villages Koodapattu will appear on the horizon. Koodapattu was known for its many rich landlords and most of them were Vellala Gounders. The village has more than 150 houses. The Jalagam parai waterfalls is the local holiday spot for the surrounding villagers.

To the South West of Koodapattu was a big fruit grove managed and run by the Tamil Nadu Government. This village has agricultural lands that are fertile round the year and harvests are bountiful. Koodapattu had one Nainathi Gounder as the elite class among its multiple castes and communities. There can be no foil to Nainaththi's word in Koodapattu village. Opposite to Nainaththi's house was the house of Srinivasa gounder, who was also well off with all the creature comforts like Tractor, Motorcycle, etc.

To the North of Koodapattu is the village of Kakkanaampalayam. Govindasami Nayakkar was the Panchayat board president of Kakkanaampalayam. Koodapattu has farmlands in the east and Nondi Palani was an ice cream vendor living there. Nondi Palani started off as a regular Communist and then turned in to a Communist extremist. He also befriended many of the Dharmapuri's Communist extremists.

Dharmapuri range Communist extremists and Jolarpet Communist extremists were recommended as farmhands by Nondi Palani in Koodapattu and neighbouring villages to spy on rich farm owners in those villages. On 22 Apr 1978 a complaint was filed by Manikka gounder on Nondi Palani and Natarasan accusing that they stole the pump set motor in his land. This cooked up complaint was fronted by Srinivasa Gounder. Communist extremists wanted to extract revenge for that untrue complaint. (Thiruppaththur taluk P.S.Cr No 294 U/S 447, 379 I.P.C.)

extremists assembled in field outhouses during night times and drew up a revenge list for killing. Even after coming to know about their attack plans, the villagers acted like that they were not concerned. The extremists worked there for more days and watched who were all the farmers that extract high loan interests, who abuse or treat their workers unfairly etc.. Then they waited for the right moment to jump in to action.

One day at 6 PM a bicycle gang started from Ponneri of Jolarpet. They took the circuitous path along the yelagiri foothills, reached Vengayapalli and merged with the bicycle gang waiting there. All of them pedalled non-stop and reached Jalagampari before nightfall. Then they waited for complete darkness to fall. At around 7 PM they parked their bicycles near the compound wall of Koodapattu Fruit Grove. Tree branches were blowing in the gentle cool breeze. They took bandannas and covered their mouths and noses to prevent others from identifying them. Their brown eyes shone with anticipation of the murderous task ahead of them and their hands tightly gripped their weapons. One Extremist climbed the Telephone pole and severed the telephone wires to prevent the news reaching Police.

They then split in to teams of three. Each team carried a flash light, a machete, and a rod. More than 10 such armed extremist teams invaded the flanks of Koodapattu and began their action. They attacked violently with weapons who ever crossed their path. Nondi Palani was carrying a flash light and was shining the flash light and showing the mob, their way forward in the all encompassing darkness.

First house to come under their attack was Nainaththi Gounder's house. Nainathi was sitting relaxedly in the porch and examining accounts in the yellow light of an incandescent bulb. The extremist team recognized Nainaththi even in that dim yellow light and chopped Nainathi in many places. Injured Nainathi let out a terrible scream filled with pain, fell down. Then they broke the bulb and darkness covered that porch. The same extremist team invaded the opposite house belonging to Srinivasa Gounder. They chased him inside his house and chopped him in many places. Srinivasan's wife begged for mercy by falling at their feet but it fell on deaf ears. They left after breaking the lights and threw Communist pamphlets at the scene of crime.

Another extremist team attacked Srinivasan's house-shed and poured petrol and set fire on his tractor and motorcycle. The 10 extremist teams advanced, entered all the streets of Koodapattu and broke all the street lights one after another. They attacked the villagers sitting in front of their houses, hit them with rods and chopped them with machetes. All the injured villagers were bleeding profusely. Srinivasa Gounder died on the spot. Nainathi's pulse was sinking.

Minutes later the extremist gang, completed their deadly assault on the village, reached the Fruit Grove from the backside of the village. Kakkanampalayam Govindsami Nayakkar was riding a bicycle saw the gang and shouted. One of the extremists hacked Govindasami Nayakkar on his head. He dropped his bicycle and fell down bleeding from his head. One of the gang member yelled "Leave him alone, Leave him alone!". The gang pulled back from Govindasami Nayakkar and started running to their parked bicycles. They hopped on their bicycles, crossed the main road, sped off and disappeared in the direction of Ponneri.

The whole village of Koodapattu gathered to help the injured ones. Nainathi's pulse showed some signs of life. The villagers took him to the Vellore Christian Medical College Hospital. They also called the fire tenders from the next village. The smoldering fire on the half burnt tractor and motorcycle were finally extinguished.

Then they informed the Police. Hearing the news, Thirupaththoor Sub Inspector Chinnarasu reached the village of Koodapattu with the Police troops. He rescued the injured fourteen men including KakkanamPalayam Govindasami Nayakkar from certain death by admitting them in time at Thirupaththoor Government Hospital.

Police conducted inquest for the already dead Srinivasa Gounder. Police also seized the notices - handwritten pamphlets using red ink - found in Srinivasa gounder's house and other places of action.

These notices carried the usual Communist Propaganda. Police sent them along with other articles seized from the scenes to the court. Thirupaththoor town police investigated this case for three days and then transferred it to Q-Branch for further investigation. Q-Branch Deputy Superintendent came from Madras. Vellore Q-Branch Inspector called Q-Branch Sub-Inspector R.Palani and Dharmapuri Sub Inspector Padmanabhan to investigate this case further.

❦ 16 ❦
Police Dragnet

The villagers managed to capture one of the extremists invaded Koodapattu that day. His name was Natarajan and he was handed over to the Thirupaththoor Taluk police. Thirupaththoor taluk police let the accused Natarajan to escape due to their carelessness. In this incident - two murders, one attempt to murder, one arson, assault at fourteen places - in total, crime had occurred in seventeen different places. Also in this incident the extremists neither used grenades nor fire crackers during attacks like that of at Vellalampatti, Nagarsampatti of Dharmapuri district.

D.S.P. Ramasami and Inspector Tagoorpal came from Madras. They joined Dharmapuri Inspector Subbannan, Sub Inspector Padmanabhan, Salem Inspector Jeyapalan, Sub Inspector Ramasami and more than 100 Armed reserve police men were called in. They were formed in to seven teams and conducted Combing Operations in midnight hours at many neighboring villages.

The teams also climbed the Yelagiri mountain and conducted their searches there as well. Villages of Kandhili, Sundarampalli, Maththoor, Odaisalpatti, Paaroor, Arasampatti, Naagarasampatti, Thirupaththoor Sugar mill, Veerapalli, Chandrapallam, Kaveripattu were marked as candidate villages for extremist hiding. The above police men were tasked by D.S.P. Ramasami to search in all the above villages. Searches were conducted at a rapid clip without delays but all the searches were unfruitful. All the extremists had exited these villages and had gone underground.

Q-Branch officers at Vellore, in particular, Inspector Henry Jospeh and Sub Inspector R.Palani were compiling historical crime records about the extremists starting from the year 1976 and were updating them with latest crimes. Once Q-Branch men got a credible tip about extremist Jeyachandran visiting his Jolarpet house on Deepavali day.

On the night before Deepavali, D.S.P. Ramasami Nadar, Tamilnadu Special Police (TSP) Inspector Munusami, Q-Branch Inspector Krishnasami, Sub Inspector R.Palani, and armed reserve men were lying in wait near the premises of Sun beedi factory. Then hours later they besieged Thangavelu Gounder's house and conducted searches inside the house. But no extremists nor their traces were found.

On a hunch they climbed the stairwell next to the house and the Q-Branch men reached the top floor of the house. There they saw the extremist Jeyachandran was blissfully in deep slumber and was sleeping through the noises that arose in the ground floor due to men searching. He was arrested and brought to the Thirupaththoor town police station. They offered him biryani for his hunger-pangs and after he dined on it, they enquired him about other extremists. But he was a hard nut to crack and refused to part with any details about his comrades. Police felt defeated and they remanded him in Thirupaththoor S.M.Court.

Extremist Ammaiyappan was living in a house near Jolarpet Railway Station and arrangements were in place to alert the police if he showed up in the area. D.M.K. Sympathizer K.K.Mani, A.D.M.K.Sympathazier K.Mani agreed to alert the police on sighting him. Following one such alert the police and Q-Branch reached his house arrested him. The Q-Branch enquired him and after enquiry he was sent to the court custody.

The next to come in to the Police net was "Kuruvi" Kanagaraj of Chandrapallam(who was killed later in a police encounter). Q-Branch Inspector Krishnasami, Sub Inspector R.Palani were following leads about his movements. They came to know of his impending visit to his house and the tip also warned that he was armed with a gun and a Grenade. The team reached the village of Chandrapallam and Q-Branch Sub Inspector R.Palani loaded his revolver with bullets and they waited. Then they entered Kuruvi's house. Kuruvi caught a whiff of the police raid, pushed the Q-Branch police aside and bolted like a lightning. The police was unable to shoot him either and later understood the significance of his nickname "Kuruvi" which means Sparrow in Tamil. He flies (i.e. runs) like a Sparrow hence his nick name.

The raids and searches were executed by multiple teams and one such team was led by Q-Branch Sub Inspector R.Palani. Besides R.Palani, the team consisted of Head constable Selvaraj, Jolarpet constable Raju, and 10 other armed reserve men. They were conducting raids in the villages near Yelagiri foothills using a police van. They all were under the guise of raiding illegal arrack distillers in an attempt to not alarm the extremists. Because of this they were able to arrest four extremists involved in Koodapattu incident in four different villages in a single day.

Q-Branch men in disguise, hid in an illegal arrack distillation factory and were watching the passers by. A marriage party was going in a procession. constable Raju pointed a person in that procession and whispered "There goes extremist Varadhan, Catch him!!!". Immediately Q-Branch Sub Inspector pounced on him and arrested. Then they packed him in their van and left the spot.

A few hours later when they were staking out in the village of Gandhi gramam they sighted the naxal Ezhumalai. They arrested him in the middle of the road. Then they were in wait near Naxal Chinnamottur Ezhumalai's house. They sighted Naxal Shanmugam who was visiting his pregnant wife and arrested him in front of his wife. Then the team went to Ramanoor and were looking out for extremists. There they sighted extremist Krishnan by chance and arrested him.

It looked like lady luck smiled on the Q-Branch team led by Sub Inspector R.Palani and they were able to arrest 4 extremists involved in Koodapattu assault in a span of 24 hours. The arrested extremists were transported by van to the Thirupaththoor Police station.

There is a strange thing to be noted in the aftermath of these continual arrests. When this raid day began, Q-Branch Sub Inspector R.Palani was preparing to leave for Madras to file an affidavit in the Madras High Court. Q-Branch Inspector from Madras - Tagoorpal - directed Palani to not to leave for Madras duty. He complained to Sub Inspector R.Palani saying "We have come from places afar for conducting raids here in these hills. But you are leaving to Madras. You should not go to Madras and you should also conduct a raid today". Hence R.Palani had to defer his original travel plans and led a team in the raids that were scheduled for that day.

Koodapattu incident was enacted by more than 30 extremists. Q-Branch investigated and found 20 names. extremists Jeyachandran, Ammaiyappan were arrested by D.S.P. Ramasami. Q-Branch Sub Inspector R.Palani arrested four of them 1.Varadhan, 2.Ezhumalai, 3.Shanmugam, 4.Krishnan on the day of the Combing operations. The other six teams raided at many other places were not able to arrest anyone. Q-Branch Sub Inspector R.Palani's arrest of four extremists delighted D.S.P. Ramasami to a great degree. But this must have irked Inspector Tagoorpal who then asked R.Palani to leave for Madras to attend High Court duty.

Unsuspecting R.Palani left immediately for Madras and turned his focus on filing of affidavits for the next three days. There were standing orders for Sub Inspectors if they were to visit Q-Branch Headquarters they were to report to Q-Branch Superintendent. So Sub Inspector R.Palani and called on the Q-Branch Superintendent of Police Mr. K. Raveendhranath I.P.S., The Q-Branch Superintendent asked R.Palani how Q-Branch works were proceeding in general. R.Palani explained to the Superintendent that only days before he arrested 4 Communist extremists - 1. Varadhan, 2. Ezhumalai, 3. Shanmugam, 4. Krishnan. He added that after arresting them he handed them over to D.S.P. Ramasami who applauded his efforts.

This news shared by Sub Inspector R.Palani angered the Superintendent visibly and he explained to R.Palani, Tagoorpal had told the Superintendent that Tagoorpal himself arrested the four extremists. Tagoorpal had since sent a request to the Superintendent in view of his accomplishment, that his name be recommended to then Inspector General of Police F.V.Arul for "Meritorious Service Entry".

The angry Superintendent ordered some men to fetch Tagoorpal to his office to hear his explanation in the matter. But information came back that Tagoorpal had gone to the High Court. So the Superintendent ordered to prepare a Reward roll for R.Palani and offered him a small amount to comfort him.

In this case, with the idea that it will be useful during identification Parades, Sub Inspector R.Palani was compiling the Bio-data of these extremists along with their mug shots. So he requested the Thirupaththoor Magistrate to order the Jail authorities to take photographs of these extremists.

Magistrate refused to issue such an order saying the law doesn't permit him. Sub Inspector R.Palani cited the following section to the Thirupaththoor Magistrate and after reading the following sections the Magistrate agreed.

THE IDENTIFICATION OF PRISONERS ACT, 1920 - Section 5 states that:

"5. Power of Magistrate to order a person to be measured or photographed.—If a Magistrate is satisfied that, for the purposes of any investigation or proceeding under the Code of Criminal Procedure, 1898 (5 of 1898) it is expedient to direct any person to allow his measurements or photograph to be taken, he may make an order to that effect, and in that case the person to whom the order relates shall be produced or shall attend at the time and place specified in the order and shall allow his measurements or photograph to be taken, as the case may be, by a police officer: Provided that no order shall be made directing any person to be photographed except by a Magistrate of the First Class: Provided further, that no order shall be made under this section unless the person has at some time been arrested in connection with such investigation or proceeding. "

The Magistrate ordered that these extremists were to be handed over to the Vellore North Police Station. When approached, Vellore North Police station Sub Inspector Perumal refused to cooperate in photographing these extremists. Q-Branch Sub Inspector R.Palani was doggedly determined to record the extremists faces by taking their photographs. So he escalated the issue to Q-Branch Superintendent in Madras, Raveendranath I.P.S. explaining this predicament over the phone. The Q-Branch Superintendent phoned Vellore Superintendent regarding this situation and sought his help. Perumal got a phone call from his superior, Superintendent of Police,Vellore, and after that Perumal cooperated in photographing the above extremists.

Sub Inspector Perumal was intially non-cooperative because he was terrified that the extremists might attack him as well his Police station. After grappling with all these obstacles Sub Inspector R.Palani finally managed to photograph the extremists. To round out the already eventful day the Naxals made funny faces while the camera trigger was pressed to prevent a proper photographic record of their visages !!

Shanthi was the name of the underground Communist extremist Sivalingam's wife. She fell in to a prolonged illness and moved from Vakkanampatti to her mother's house in Vaniyambadi. She underwent treatment there for many months but was not cured. In 1978 Shanthi died in spite of all the medical treatment. Sivalingam was intimated by his relatives about Shanthi's death.

Q-Branch was also in receipt of this news. Q-Branch Inspector Krishnasami, Sub Inspector R.Palani, and more than ten constables were in disguise, kept a watch on the funeral near their house. But there was no sign of Sivalingam's visit to finally see the face of his wife. Q-Branch returned back to their duties empty handed.

A few days later when the Q-Branch men were in Jolarpet they heard a shocking news that indeed Sivalingam came to his wife's funeral. Since Sivalingam was told that the Q-Branch was waiting for his arrival in front of his house, he simply took an alternate route. A nearby house to where the wife's body was in rest was a Muslim family's house. Sivalingam entered that house wearing a burka and took the stairs to the top floor. There he jumped to the top floor of his house and climbed down to see his wife's body. He then spoke to his relatives for some time and took the same route out of the house.

All this happened right under the nose of the Police. Since the house was in a Muslim area there were many Muslim women and the Police did not bother checking burka wearing women.

Extremists Jeyachandran, Ammaiyappan arrested by Q-Branch D.S.P. Ramasami Nadar were imprisoned in Vellore Central Jail. Q-Branch Sub Inspector R.Palani arrested four extremists i.e. - Varadhan, Ezhumalai, Shanmugam, Krishnan - were also in the same Vellore Central Jail. These six accused were filing bail petitions in

Madras High Court every 15 days non-stop. To counter these petitions Sub Inspector R.Palani had to travel to Madras and stayed there two days every week. He prepared and filed affidavits in the Madras High Court regarding these six accused for months on end.

This affidavit carried the depositions of the eye witness(162 Cr.P.C) proving that these accused were indeed guilty and requested to dismiss their bail petitions. The Court asked to submit many documents pertaining to the Koodapattu case and after studying them the judges many times dismissed the bail petitions of the above accused. This tug-of-war continued for around a year and the accused were behind the bars without bail all the while.

A renowned Communist lawyer who was practicing in the Madras High Court by the name of K.V.Shankaran filed a petition in the Madras High Court concerning these accused. In that he explained that the Q-Branch Police accused six men as involved in the Koodapattu case and keeping them in prison for years, which was against the law. So he requested in his petition that they should be released forthwith. His petition came for hearing before the honorable Justice C.J.R. Paul.

Lawyer Shankaran argued that the six men were accused for murder. The case has to be conducted in the Sessions Court. According to Indian Criminal Procedure Code only the judge who tries this case can alone extend the remand period of the accused. But Thirupaththoor Sub

Magistrate who was not allowed by the law to conduct the trial in this case had extended the remand for more than a year. Hence extending their remand was an instance of wrongful confinement. And the involved officers should be punished and the six accused should be released forthwith.

"IPC Section 341:Punishment for wrongful restraint
Whoever wrongfully restrains any person shall be punished with simple imprisonment for a term which may extend to one month, or with fine which may extend to five hundred rupees, or with both.

IPC Section 342:Punishment for wrongful confinement
Whoever wrongfully confines any person shall be punished with simple imprisonment of either description for a term which may extend to one year, or with fine which may extend to one thousand rupees, or with both.

IPC Section 343:Wrongful confinement for three or more days
Whoever wrongfully confines any person for three days or more, shall be punished with imprisonment of either description for a term which may extend to two years, or with fine, or with both.

IPC Section 344:Wrongful confinement for ten or more days
Whoever wrongfully confines any person for ten days, or more, shall be punished with imprisonment of either

description for a term which may extend to three years, and shall also be liable to fine.

IPC Section 345:Wrongful confinement of person for whose liberation writ has been issued
Whoever keeps any person in wrongful confinement, knowing that a writ for the liberation of that person has been duly issued, shall be punished with imprisonment of either description for a term which may extend to two years."

He cited a favorable judgment of Andhra High Court in a similar case and read the judgment aloud in front of the court. After reading he tossed the thick legal tome on the wooden desk with a big thud. Other lawyers present in the Court were speechless. It was considered as a big bomb dropped on the entire Police force.

Justice Paul called the Assistant Public prosecutor for his arguments. But the Assistant Public Prosecutor Karpaga Vinayagam was a freshman in the High Court cases. Since he was unable to present the legal nuances in this case Justice ordered him to discuss with his superior and come and argue the next day. When Karpaga Vinayagam explained the situation to his Senior Public Prosecutor Raja Manikkam, he looked condescendingly at Karpaga Vinayagam and exclaimed "This is a trifling case. Do I have to appear even for this case?"

The next day Raja Manikkam appeared before Justice Paul and began his argument. As per old Cr.P.C in a

Sessions trial case they used to conduct a Preliminary Trial in the lower court. Since it was causing delays, in the new Cr.P.C in 1973 they removed the procedure of Preliminary Trial. Instead it was stipulated that witness depositions, seized articles, were to be organized and it is sufficient to send them along with the F.I.R. to the Sessions court.

Hence in the lower Court, Judge examines all the submitted documents and decides if they are sufficient for a trial, and after that they allot a P.R.C. number and send the case to a higher Court. These activities of the lower court can be considered equivalent to a Preliminary Trial.

Raja Manikkam further added that trying to use this loop hole for the advantage of the criminals is an offence in itself. The Court was adjourned to the next day for Judgment.

In his eighteen page judgment, Justice Paul examined and analysed the arguments of both the parties and concluded that perusal of documents in the lower court is deemed equivalent to a Preliminary Trial. He awarded the case to the Police side.

The Police side heaved a big sigh of relief and rejoiced.

~ 17 ~
Investigation

After Koodapattu assault, Kakkanaam palayam Govindasami Nayakkar started cooperating with the Q-Branch and local police in a big way. He alerted all his contacts in these villages and was aggressively gathering information on Communist extremists. He collected useful information with the help of his fellow party members in Ponneri circle, Jolarpet circle and many adjacent villages. He passed on such information without any delays to the Q-Branch D.S.P. Ramasami so that they can act on such information immediately. Because of his cooperation Police came to know about many hitherto unknown Criminals and extremists in these areas.

The extremists also came to know that Govindasami Nayakkar was acting as an informant to the police. Hence they decided to take him out. Govindasami Nayakkar came to know about their plans from his sources. So he built a big hut near the peepul tree and Periyaandavar temple at the entrance to the village. In that hut, Nayakkar lodged ten youngsters to protect him day and night, and counter attack the extremists. The daily needs of these men were looked after by Nayakkar and they were to shower if needed in the near by Panchayath board office. Extremists now were unable to touch the Nayakkar.

After extremists understood the prevailing situation that Govindasami Nayakkar cannot be attacked in his village

Kakkanaam palayam, they decided to shift the attack location to Koodapattu itself. Three months after, one sunny day Govindasami Nayakkar was waiting for the bus at a bus stop in Koodapattu. A disguised extremist gang jumped out and raced to attack Govindasami Nayakkar with dangerous weapons like machetes. The villagers present at the bus stop, blocked the attack and chased down the extremist gang. The extremist gang entered the thick corn fields east of the main road. From there they activated a grenade and hurled at the villagers.

Unfortunately for the extremists, the grenade thrown by them failed to explode. In their excitement the villagers could not recognize this attack or the dangers of a grenade explosion. Since the grenade they threw turned out to be a dud, the extremists receded deep in to the corn fields and disappeared. Thirupaththoor Taluk police registered an F.I.R. (Thiruppaththur Taluk P.S.Cr No 745/1977 U/S 307 I.P.C.) and investigated. The story did not end there.

The very next day Q-Branch Sub Inspector R.Palani arrived at the crime scene. He examined over it inch by inch for clues. There next to the main road was a Pillai Marutham tree. Near the tree was lying a lone grenade made out of lead. Sub Inspector R.Palani cordoned off the immediate area near the un-exploded grenade and informed his higher ups in Madras.

Upon close examination, the grenade was found to be carrying these markings in white - "MADE IN CHINA".

This was a solid evidence obtained for the first time confirming the fact that China was supplying grenades to the extremists. A team of explosive experts arrived from Ashok Nagar, Madras and examined the grenade for further clues. They identified it as a powerful grenade and defused it safely.

❧ 18 ❦
Wineyards

Since the police raids had become a daily feature in the villages in and around Jolarpet, Communist extremists picked a new spot for their planning activities. The name of the new village was Kuppam. Kuppam is relatively unknown village in the Southernmost Andhra. They met in the secluded groves in and around Kuppam and schemed about their future attacks. Natrampalli is located in the Northernmost part of Tamil Nadu. To the North of Natrampalli is Karnataka and to its East is Andhra. Between Natrampalli and Kuppam is the Kothur Reserve Forest.

The overflowing waters of Karnataka's Petha Managalam Lake and the brook from Kuppam Hills merge together and enter Tamil Nadu border as River Palar. This River Palar irrigates agricultural lands in Pachur. In the Pachur Foothills, the cash crop of grapes were cultivated widely. Many grape varieties like Kabul grapes, Panneer grapes, Green grapes, Seedless sweet grapes were cultivated by the farmers here.

In Pachur and in the Hills of Andhra border, Custard Apples, Sappottas, rare scarlet fleshed Rama Custard Apples were predominantly grown. In the valleys, small brinjals with thorns were cultivated. Near the Railway gate, the wholesale merchants will be auctioning off baskets and baskets of these fruits and brinjals. Since there are two railway gates one after the other, if these gates once closed, they will remain closed at least one and half an hour. In the intermittent time, passengers in the buses destined for Andhra and Karnataka used to disembark. They will stretch their legs and relax while eating Custard apples, Sappottas, Bananas, and Tender coconuts. Then they will resume with their journeys once the gates are thrown open.

Govindasami Chettiyar a native of these foothills, owned more than ten acres of fertile lands. Instead of cultivating paddy, banana, sugarcane in these lands he wanted to see easy money and so he was cultivating grapes. This cashcrop doesn't require that many farmhands also. So the Communists opposed Govindasami Chettiyar openly.

Once a Communist extremist by the name of Kannamani, came in person and threatened Govindasami asking money. Kannamani was wearing a dhothi and was carrying a machete conspicuously. Govindasami Chettiyar intimated the Natrampalli police about these threats. At that time Police were in receipt of information that Communist extremists were seeking extortion money from big land owners and rice mill owners. The extremists were in need of money to augment their party in more villages. So they were sending extortion letters demanding money. But Govindasami Chettiyar refused to part with the money demanded by them.

Extremist Kannamani and a few others joined up and planned to hack Govindasami to death. One day Govindasami as usual paid the workers who pruned the grape leaves and was returning home. He was ambushed on his way home by extremists led by Kannamani. Govindasami Chettiyar sustained deep wounds and gashes on his face and limbs. The villagers gathered and gave the extremists a chase. But they ran and disappeared.

The injured Chettiyar was loaded in a van and taken to the Christian Medical Hospital in Vellore and was admitted in the Intensive Care Unit. After one month intensive treatment fortunately Govindasami Chettiyar recovered from his wounds.

In the mean while, there was an exodus of Communist extremists in the Ponneri circle and they scattered to distant places. But many Communist sympathizers remained behind and were causing troubles to the big land owners. Chakravarthy was an important informer of these underground comrades. In Ponneri circle, Bakthavachalam Reddiyar appealed to the villagers about this Communists' informer Chakravarthy. Some youngsters in Ponneri gathered together and tied this Chakravarthy to a tree and beat him to death. These youngsters were led by one Durai.

19
Practice Makes Perfect

In the village of Koodapattu there lived a Chinnasamy who was blind in both the eyes. He was regularly gathering information about Communist extremists and was passing those to the Q-Branch. The extremists slayed both Ponneri Durai and Koodapattu Chinnasami in cold blood. Q-Branch personnel from Vellore were shocked to hear about these two incidents. Even a blind man could not escape the indiscriminate wrath of these murderers.

The above Chakravarthy was caught hold of Q-Branch Sub Inspector R.Palani roughly one month before his death and was brought to a photo studio next to Golden lodge in Jolarpet. R.Palani completed his bio-data and along with his photographs, sent it to the Q-Branch headquarters in Madras.

To exact revenge for this Chakravarthy's death the extremists now targeted Bakthavachchalam Reddiyar. The Reddiyar came to know about this threat and applied to the Vellore district Collector for a gun license and then purchased a foreign made revolver. Reddiyar showed his new weapon to Q-Branch Sub Inspector R.Palani and boasted that no one will be able to touch him now.

Sub Inspector R.Palani opened his vest, displaying his personal fire arm and told him that he remains armed with a gun always. R.Palani advised him that it is not sufficient if one merely keeps a hand gun on his person.

While "Pulling the trigger" is very simple in concept, it creates problems for most shooters, even experienced ones.

A good practitioner of shooting should also learn how to clean the fire-arm, be aware of the expiry date of the bullets, etc. He further added to pick a desolate shooting practice area like a mountain and practice his aim and only then a firearm will be useful to him.

Bakthavachchala Reddiyar even after listening to his timely advise failed to learn shooting. He kept a handful of bullets in one side pocket of his "Jippa" and the firearm in the other side pocket while wandering through the narrow streets of his native village.

Many months rolled by and on 30 May 1979, Q-Branch Sub Inspector R.Palani was promoted to the post of Inspector in Tamil Nadu Special Branch C.I.D. and had to relocate to the city of Madras. The post he held in Q-Branch remained vacant for many years without any successors.

20

Blood Lands

Three of the Naxals sustained only slightly injuries. These three Naxals jumped out of the vehicle and disappeared in the darkness. (Thiruppaththur Town P.S Cr No 572/1980 U/S 302 I.P.C and 307 I.P.C R/W 286 I.P.C.)

No information on the escaped three Naxals who were injured can be found. But it was reported later they got their wounds treated with the help of a sidha doctor.

A few weeks later, Communist lawyer Bakthavachchalam published some advertisements stating that Communist leaders of Tamil Nadu will arrive on a particular day to Thirupaththoor to inquire about the death of Inspector Palanisami and four other constables.

The day advertised by Bakthavachchalam came. More than twenty Communists came and stayed at lawyer Bakthavachchalam's house. The public were livid that these Communists struck our Inspector and constables dead in our town itself. The public were seething what else these Communists were going to inquire about now. More than 500 general public assembled in front of Bakthavachchalam's house. Their anger finally boiled over when some of them barged in to the house and attacked the Communists staying there. The wounded Communists ran to save their lives and caught buses plying out of Thirupaththoor and disappeared from the scene.

Some of these Communists went straight to the city of Madras and reached the M.L.A. Hostel. There they complained about the attack, on them to the Communist M.L.A.s. Doctors were called in to the M.L.A. Hostel and the injured Communists were treated there.

The public back in Thirupththoor when the Communists escaped they turned their anger at Bakthavachchalam's house which was ransacked and destroyed. Bakthavachchalam vacated Thirupaththoor and relocated to Madras. He started practicing his legal profession in the Madras High Court.

The Thirupaththoor range police men were happy to hear this news and said good riddance.

21
Peace Returns

The Tamil Nadu Government appointed a new Director General of Police (D.I.G.) for the Vellore district. The new D.I.G. raised a memorial for the deceased Inspector Palanisami and four other constables in the premises of Thirupaththoor town police station. August 6th of every year is observed as a remembrance day by the Police men.

The new D.I.G. established the informers throughout this area and smashed the Naxal violence with his iron hands. Higher officials in the Tamil Nadu Police department respected his judgment and accepted his suggestions whole-heartedly.

Tamil Nadu people along with the police personnel will fondly remember the courageous actions of the D.I.G.

People of Tamil Nadu and Police personnel eagerly look forward to the creation of future police officers with the same caliber. This is the unalloyed truth!

Can you guess the name of that Deputy Inspector General of Police ?

Our Beloved Walter Daavaram I.P.S. !!!

22
Plight Of C.I.D.

"An army marches on its stomach"

- Napoleon Bonaparte

One Inspector, one Sub Inspector, one Head constable, one constable was the strength of Q-Branch C.I.D. allotted for a district. Reader should not assume that Q-Branch personnel were given facilities and resources on par with International secret agents or even to fictional characters like James Bond. In Tamil Nadu, none of the Q-Branch personnel except Sub Inspector R.Palani possessed a small arm like a revolver or pistol for their safety.

Reason being the officers were afraid if they happen to loose the fire-arm, they might be dismissed from the Police force. This was the prevailing state of secret police in Tamil Nadu. The author feels that he must register the following situations to effectively portray the real state of secret police in Tamil Nadu.

We read about the stabbing of Ambur writer Desingu in the preceding chapters. The immediate reaction of Tamil Nadu Police department to this incident was all the Police personnel in Vellore Q-Branch - lock, stock and barrel were transferred to Thirupaththoor permanently. So the Q-Branch personnel had to leave behind their families in Vellore and they were forced to stay and work in Thirupaththoor for years on end.

In Madras some Naxals were involved in Radio station attack and bus burning attacks, Pennadam murders. Police were on the lookout for them. So to handle this emergent threat the Tamil Nadu Government issued an order to begin Q-Branch in all the district headquarters. In 1975, as per that order, a Q-Branch Inspector was appointed in all the districts.

Then a Sub Inspector, a Head constable and a constable were added to the district Q-Branch. Many of these positions remained vacant. The district Q-Branches were started only in name, because they weren't provided with any facilities like buildings, communication facilities like phone or wireless, or even transportation facility like a car or a jeep. The above Q-Branch personnel worked in these threadbare conditions for ten years.

The situation for the Vellore Q-Branch was also the same. The Vellore Q-Branch personnel were relegated to using the house of Inspector Henry Joseph. Except the Inspector rest of the personnel had to sit only on the floor. When they were suddenly transferred to Thirupaththoor even that was not possible. Where ever they stay the night, sometimes in old lodges, that room will become that days' Q-Branch office. This was the situation of Q-Branch in Thirupaththoor.

In 1976 one sovereign Gold shot up suddenly from rupees 200 to rupees 400. Q-Branch personnel were unable to rent (daily or monthly) a room or a house for staying the nights. Reason was, the room rent for one person became 6 rupees and for a month 180 rupees.

For one person to have an ordinary breakfast was minimum 50 paise. Lunch was minimum 1 rupee 50 paise. Dinner was 50 paise. For tea...etc., 50 paise. In total food expenses for one person amounted to minimum 180 Rupees per month.

For food and lodging it took minimum 360 Rupees per month per person. A maximum amount of Rs 120 was given as traveling allowance to a Sub Inspector and Rs 80 to a Head constable.

A monthly shortage of Rs 240 stared bleakly at a Sub Inspector leaving him to wonder if it was all a grim joke by the police department. Amidst all the work related challenges, it added one more challenge of managing this monetary shortage...!

As if this was not enough, Inspectors, Sub Inspectors, and Head constables from far off districts like Salem, Coimbatore and even Kanniyakumari were called in for Q-Branch duty to help in conducting searches and investigations. D.S.P.s will not stay for more than 5 days and will return to Madras. S.P.s wont even stay for more than a day. Only the officers below that levels bore the full brunt of this financial shortage situation.

These officers were ordered to travel daily to a different district, search in two to three villages, conduct investigations and all of these were to be done travelling by bus or by foot. Even if you travel in buses, you must get down at the bus stops and walk the rest of the distance. Hence the Q-Branch personnel had to walk at least 15 KM per day.

In all these villages, for the visiting Q-Branch personnel the villagers are new, their habits, customs even dialects were different. The Q-Branch personnel had to improvise a lot in gaining the trust of these villagers. Even if the villagers trust these Q-Branch personnel, to extract useful information from them is like sighting of a Unicorn. The Q-Branch personnel handled these challenges successfully and gathered useful information.

They are supplied with only bus warrants. Where ever they happen to go they had to see to their food and lodging. Once they were journeying to a remote village called Ayuthakalam in Trichy to interrogate some arrested Naxals. They reached Trichy around midnight and at a non-descript place they decided to spend that night. They were unable to sleep due to rampant Mosquitoes buzzing overhead and bites. Some how they slept for couple of hours.

Suddenly all hell broke loose as there were ten to fifteen buses surrounding them and blaring their horns. The men jumped up to their feet and in their sleep induced confusion they were not able to get their bearings quickly. Finally they realized it was still dark but early morning hours and they had chosen to stay the night in the middle of a bus stand !!

That's all the sleep they got that day and had to continue their journey. This is how most night stays ended up for Q-Branch personnel. They were unable to stay even in Traveler's Bungalows. There were no Travelers' Bungalows at places where they were going. For morning showers they had no choice but to use street taps of those hamlets.

Vellore Q-Branch Sub Inspector and Head constable were teamed up with Dharmapuri Sub Inspector Padmanabha Iyer for a secret mission. The three of them were unable to find any decent place to stay the nights. So they had to stay in a Chettiyar's Rice Mill located in the outskirts of Thirupaththoor. Their assignment dragged on for months and so was their rice mill night stays.

This particular rice mill had no lavatory or facility to take baths. The three of them were subjected to the hardship of performing their morning ablutions in an open ground next to the rice mill - for months. This open ground was infested with Cobras and fire ants and they had to get used to these dangerous visitors while relieving themselves !!

They bathed in a pump-set near by the well. Washing their dirty clothes were done there as well.

Whichever village they are in that day for conducting investigations, the stale and sour "Kuzhi Paniyaram", "Bonda", "Vadai" available in village petty shops formed the mainstay of their lunch. Even ordinary Idlis wont be available in these villages. Inspite of their spartan meals, they faced money shortages every month. That is the moment, the name "Kakkanaam palayam Govindasami Nayakkar" will flash in their minds.

If one goes to his tiled house, you can get - A day old rice gruel or ragi gruel for free. Some times they will get good food as well. Govindasami Nayakkar felt sorry seeing the Q-Branch personnel suffer in hunger. If they reach his house past lunch hours, Nayakkar will call the petty shop owner and ask to make bondas and vadais and Nayakkar will offer that to them. To satisfy their hunger pangs they will be forced to accept those snacks as their lunch.

If the searches are scheduled in hamlets, groves and hills - Starvation will be the name of the game. In freezing temperatures many nights had to be spent in conducting "Lurking Patrols" at the Foothills of Yelagiri. Situations like walking while drenched in rain fall arose many times too. There were no hills left unclimbed, no villages not treaded upon, in the districts of Dharmapuri and Thirpupaththoor.

Back in those times, there were no mobile phones or google maps. Even rotary dial phones were rarely present - only one lonely phone per village was not unusual. Who stays in which location, where they spend their nights, how they manage to eat - such questions were never asked by the higher officials to the field personnel. Not even one day!! The higher officials never asked nor arranged even for the basic amenities of the field personnel.

Higher officials will be accompanying the low level personnel throughout the day. After waking up in the morning at 8 AM, the first thing higher officials feigning ignorance will ask "What was the progress yesterday?".

Independence Day, Gandhi Jayanthi, Republic Day, Pongal, Deepavali were marked as occasions with high risk of Naxal attacks and Police personnel will be forced to work on that day too. One cannot even visit his family at his native place on the salary day as well.

Thirupaththoor Q-Branch Inspector was a constable rank promoted to Inspector post. They had to depend on the Sub Inspector for the reason that - Daily Situation Report and High Court attendance were all to be composed in English. So they will think the Sub Inspector should always be present within their calling distance. They won't even sanction leaves. Even if the D.S.P. sanctions leave for the Sub Inspector, the Inspector will hesitate to let him go on leave to visit his family.

This was how the Q-Branch functioned from 1975 to 1979 in a continual state of emergency. In the Ambur writer Desingu stabbing case the accused were identified after much hardships. Rewards for the personnel who cracked that case were not even offered by the higher officials. "All glory goes to the God !!!" must have been their policy !!!

"Amateurs talk about Tactics, but professionals discuss Logistics"
    - General Robert H. Barrow, US Marine Corps.

The above quote and the name of our ancestral king Perunsotru Uthiyan Cheralathan only comes to the mind.

Q-Branch officers based on a hunch, called for the father of Seeralan to identify his body. That act should have been rewarded. But the I.A.S. officers not only didn't bother to enquire about the Q-Branch personnel's contributions but they went so far to suspend the Inspector and constables. Why?

Even the general public who were panic stricken from the Naxal attacks praised the Police actions. But these I.A.S. officers deliberately inculpated the Q-Branch personnel and insulted them awarding suspensions etc. I.A.S. officers had to cower to none, since they were the Executive magistrate themselves. Inspite of receiving proper justifications why they failed to uphold the Police cause? Instead they resorted to insulting the Q-Branch personnel.

Amidst all the above challenges the Q-Branch personnel managed to deliver tangible results in time. Those tireless efforts of the Q-Branch personnel ought to be praised without any reservations.

Photos of the author in the period : 1979-80

Uniformed

Plain Clothed

ಬು END ଓଃ

www.ingramcontent.com/pod-product-compliance
Lightning Source LLC
Chambersburg PA
CBHW030706220526
45463CB00005B/1934